100 POEMS
BY
100 POETS

100 POEMS
— BY —
100 POEMS

AN ANTHOLOGY

selected by
HAROLD PINTER,
GEOFFREY GODBERT
and
ANTHONY ASTBURY

Grove Press
New York

First published in Great Britain in 1986
by Methuen London and Grenville Press.
Printed in the United States of America

Library of Congress Cataloging-in-Publication Data

100 poems by 100 poets.
1. English poetry. 2. American poetry.   I. Pinter, Harold,
1930–   .   II. Godbert, Geoffrey.   III. Astbury, Anthony.
IV. Title: One hundred poems by one hundred poets.
PR1174.A12   1987   821'.008   87-206
ISBN 0-8021-3279-0 (pbk.)

Grove Press
841 Broadway
New York, NY 10003

99 00 01 02   15 14 13 12 11 10 9 8 7 6 5

For George, Elspeth, Nessie
and in memory of W.S. Graham

Contents

Acknowledgements

The editors are grateful to the copyright holders listed below for permission to include the following poems.

"Sonnet" from *The Collected Poems of James Agee*, edited by Robert Fitzgerald. Copyright © 1962, 1968 by The James Agee Trust. Reprinted by permission of Houghton Mifflin Company.

"In Memory of W. B. Yeats" from *W. H. Auden: Collected Poems*, edited by Edward Mendelson. Copyright © 1940 and renewed 1968 by W. H. Auden. Reprinted by permission of Random House, Inc.

"Dream Song 4" from *The Dream Songs* by John Berryman. Copyright © 1959, 1962, 1963, 1964 by John Berryman. Reprinted by permission of Farrar, Straus and Giroux, Inc.

"Parliament Hill Fields" from *Collected Poems* by John Betjeman. Reprinted by permission of John Murray (Publishers) Ltd.

"The Fish" from *The Complete Poems* by Elizabeth Bishop. Copyright © 1983 by Alice Helen Methfessel. Copyright © 1940 by Elizabeth Bishop. Renewal copyright © 1967, 1968, 1971, 1973, 1974, 1975, 1976, 1979 by Elizabeth Bishop. Renewal copyright © 1980 by Alice Helen Methfessel. Reprinted by permission of Farrar, Straus and Giroux, Inc.

"The Unpredictable" from *A Smell of Burning* by Thomas Blackburn. Putnam and Co.

"next to of course god america i" from *IS 5* by E. E. Cummings. Copyright © 1985 by E. E. Cummings Trust. Copyright © 1926 by Horace Liveright. Copyright 1954 by E.E. Cummings. Copyright © 1985 by George James Firmage. Reprinted by permission of Liveright Publishing Corporation.

"La Figlia Che Piange" from *Collected Poems 1909–1962* by T. S. Eliot. Copyright © 1936 by Harcourt Brace Jovanovich, Inc.; copyright © 1963, 1964 by T. S. Eliot. Reprinted by permission of the publisher.

"Let it go" from *Collected Poems of William Empson*. Copyright © 1949, 1977 by William Empson. Reprinted by permission of Harcourt Brace Jovanovich, Inc.

Introduction

This book took final shape on a train journey to Cornwall in January this year, when Anthony Astbury, Geoffrey Godbert and myself went to visit Nessie Graham, following the death of her husband, W. S. Graham. By the time we had taken the return journey to London, *100 Poems by 100 Poets* was well on its way. It was a great twelve hours.

We consider each poem here to be representative of the poet's finest work: this is not necessarily to say 'the best', or the most famous. Although our final decisions were unanimous, we argued fiercely before reaching them and have no doubt our readers, faced with the results, will do the same.

These were the rules we drew up: the poems should be written in English; they should be reprinted in full; we should exclude living poets, since we needed to make our choice from the total *corpus* of each poet's work.

Arranging the poems alphabetically was an exciting experiment. I think it works.

Harold Pinter
London, April, 1986

JAMES AGEE

1909-1955

So it begins. Adam is in his earth

So it begins. Adam is in his earth
Tempted, and fallen, and his doom made sure
Oh, in the very instant of his birth:
Whose deathly nature must all things endure.
The hungers of his flesh, and mind, and heart,
That governed him when he was in the womb,
These ravenings multiply in every part:
And shall release him only to the tomb.
Meantime he works the earth, and builds up nations,
And trades, and wars, and learns, and worships chance,
And looks to God, and weaves the generations
Which shall his many hungerings advance
When he is sunken dead among his sins.
Adam is in this earth. So it begins.

MATTHEW ARNOLD
1822–1888

Dover Beach

The sea is calm to-night.
The tide is full, the moon lies fair
Upon the straits; – on the French coast the light
Gleams and is gone; the cliffs of England stand,
Glimmering and vast, out in the tranquil bay.
Come to the window, sweet is the night-air!
Only, from the long line of spray
Where the sea meets the moon-blanch'd land,
Listen! you hear the grating roar
Of pebbles which the waves draw back, and fling,
At their return, up the high strand,
Begin, and cease, and then again begin,
With tremulous cadence slow, and bring
The eternal note of sadness in.

Sophocles long ago
Heard it on the Aegean, and it brought
Into his mind the turbid ebb and flow
Of human misery; we
Find also in the sound a thought,
Hearing it by this distant northern sea.

The Sea of Faith
Was once, too, at the full, and round earth's shore
Lay like the folds of a bright girdle furl'd.

But now I only hear
Its melancholy, long, withdrawing roar,
Retreating, to the breath
Of the night-wind, down the vast edges drear
And naked shingles of the world.

Ah, love, let us be true
To one another! for the world, which seems
To lie before us like a land of dreams,
So various, so beautiful, so new,
Hath really neither joy, nor love, nor light,
Nor certitude, nor peace, nor help for pain;
And we are here as on a darkling plain
Swept with confused alarms of struggle and flight,
Where ignorant armies clash by night.

W.H. AUDEN
1907-1973

In Memory of W. B. Yeats
(d. Jan. 1939)

i

He disappeared in the dead of winter:
The brooks were frozen, the airports almost deserted,
And snow disfigured the public statues;
The mercury sank in the mouth of the dying day.
What instruments we have agree
The day of his death was a dark cold day.

Far from his illness
The wolves ran on through the evergreen forests,
The peasant river was untempted by the fashionable quays;
By mourning tongues
The death of the poet was kept from his poems.

But for him it was his last afternoon as himself,
An afternoon of nurses and rumours;
The provinces of his body revolted,
The squares of his mind were empty,
Silence invaded the suburbs,
The current of his feeling failed; he became his admirers.

Now he is scattered among a hundred cities
And wholly given over to unfamiliar affections,
To find his happiness in another kind of wood
And be punished under a foreign code of conscience.
The words of a dead man
Are modified in the guts of the living.

But in the importance and noise of to-morrow
When the brokers are roaring like beasts on the floor of the
                Bourse,
And the poor have the sufferings to which they are fairly
                accustomed,
And each in the cell of himself is almost convinced of his
                freedom,
A few thousand will think of this day
As one thinks of a day when one did something slightly
                unusual.
What instruments we have agree
The day of his death was a dark cold day.

ii

You were silly like us; your gift survived it all:
The parish of rich women, physical decay,
Yourself. Mad Ireland hurt you into poetry.
Now Ireland has her madness and her weather still,
For poetry makes nothing happen: it survives
In the valley of its making where executives
Would never want to tamper, flows on south
From ranches of isolation and the busy griefs,
Raw towns that we believe and die in; it survives,
A way of happening, a mouth.

5

iii

Earth, receive an honoured guest:
William Yeats is laid to rest.
Let the Irish vessel lie
Emptied of its poetry.

In the nightmare of the dark
All the dogs of Europe bark,
And the living nations wait,
Each sequestered in its hate;

Intellectual disgrace
Stares from every human face,
And the seas of pity lie
Locked and frozen in each eye.

Follow, poet, follow right
To the bottom of the night,
With your unconstraining voice
Still persuade us to rejoice;

With the farming of a verse
Make a vineyard of the curse,
Sing of human unsuccess
In a rapture of distress;

In the deserts of the heart
Let the healing fountain start,
In the prison of his days
Teach the free man how to praise.

APHRA BEHN
1640-1689

A thousand martyrs I have made

A thousand martyrs I have made,
  All sacrific'd to my desire;
A thousand beauties have betray'd,
  That languish in resistless fire.
The untam'd heart to hand I brought,
And fixed the wild and wandering thought.

I never vow'd nor sigh'd in vain
  But both, tho' false, were well receiv'd.
The fair are pleas'd to give us pain,
  And what they wish is soon believ'd.
And tho' I talk'd of wounds and smart,
Love's pleasures only touched my heart.

Alone the glory and the spoil
  I always laughing bore away;
The triumphs, without pain or toil,
  Without the hell, the heav'n of joy.
And while I thus at random rove
Despis'd the fools that whine for love.

JOHN BERRYMAN
1914-1972

Dream Song 4

Filling her compact & delicious body
with chicken páprika, she glanced at me
twice.
Fainting with interest, I hungered back
and only the fact of her husband & four other people
kept me from springing on her

or falling at her little feet and crying
'You are the hottest one for years of night
Henry's dazed eyes
have enjoyed, Brilliance.' I advanced upon
(despairing) my spumoni. – Sir Bones: is stuffed,
de world, wif feeding girls.

– Black hair, complexion Latin, jewelled eyes
downcast . . . The slob beside her   feasts . . . What
                                                      wonders is
she sitting on, over there?
The restaurant buzzes. She might as well be on Mars.
Where did it all go wrong? There ought to be a law
                                        against Henry.
– Mr Bones: there is.

JOHN BETJEMAN
1906–1984

Parliament Hill Fields

Rumbling under blackened girders, Midland, bound for
                                                    Cricklewood,
Puffed its sulphur to the sunset where that Land of Laundries
                                                    stood.
Rumble under, thunder over, train and tram alternate go,
Shake the floor and smudge the ledger, Charrington, Sells,
                                                    Dale and Co.,
Nuts and nuggets in the window, trucks along the lines
                                                    below.

When the Bon Marché was shuttered, when the feet were
                                                    hot and tired,
Outside Charrington's we waited, by the 'STOP HERE IF
                                                    REQUIRED',
Launched aboard the shopping basket, sat precipitately
                                                    down,
Rocked past Zwanziger the baker's, and the terrace blackish
                                                    brown,
And the curious Anglo-Norman parish church of Kentish
                                                    Town.

Till the tram went over thirty, sighting terminus again,
Past municipal lawn tennis and the bobble-hanging plane;
Soft the light suburban evening caught our ashlar-speckled
                                                    spire,
Eighteen-sixty Early English, as the mighty elms retire
Either side of Brookfield Mansions flashing fine French-
                                              window fire.

Oh the after-tram-ride quiet, when we heard a mile beyond,
Silver music from the bandstand, barking dogs by Highgate
                                                    Pond;
Up the hill where stucco houses in Virginia creeper drown –
And my childish wave of pity, seeing children carrying
                                                    down
Sheaves of drooping dandelions to the courts of Kentish
                                                    Town.

The Fish

I caught a tremendous fish
and held him beside the boat
half out of water, with my hook
fast in a corner of his mouth.
He didn't fight.
He hadn't fought at all.
He hung a grunting weight,
battered and venerable
and homely. Here and there
his brown skin hung in strips
like ancient wallpaper,
and its pattern of darker brown
was like wallpaper:
shapes like full-blown roses
stained and lost through age.
He was speckled with barnacles,
fine rosettes of lime,
and infested
with tiny white sea-lice,
and underneath two or three
rags of green weed hung down.
While his gills were breathing in
the terrible oxygen
 – the frightening gills,
fresh and crisp with blood,

that can cut so badly –
I thought of the coarse white flesh
packed in like feathers,
the big bones and the little bones,
the dramatic reds and blacks
of his shiny entrails,
and the pink swim-bladder
like a big peony.
I looked into his eyes
which were far larger than mine
but shallower, and yellowed,
the irises backed and packed
with tarnished tinfoil
seen through the lenses
of old scratched isinglass.
They shifted a little, but not
to return my stare.
– It was more like the tipping
of an object toward the light.
I admired his sullen face,
the mechanism of his jaw,
and then I saw
that from his lower lip
– if you could call it a lip –
grim, wet, and weaponlike,
hung five old pieces of fish-line,
or four and a wire leader
with the swivel still attached,
with all their five big hooks
grown firmly in his mouth.
A green line, frayed at the end
where he broke it, two heavier lines,

and a fine black thread
still crimped from the strain and snap
when it broke and he got away.
Like medals with their ribbons
frayed and wavering,
a five-haired beard of wisdom
trailing from his aching jaw.
I stared and stared
and victory filled up
the little rented boat,
from the pool of bilge
where oil had spread a rainbow
around the rusted engine
to the bailer rusted orange,
the sun-cracked thwarts,
the oarlocks on their strings,
the gunnels – until everything
was rainbow, rainbow, rainbow!
And I let the fish go.

THOMAS BLACKBURN
1916-1977

The Unpredictable

The raw and overwhelming danger
Of the first grief and the first hunger,
Too much, I dare say, to be caught
By a child's heartbeat and his thought.

Mercifully, though, from too much violence
There is oblivion and silence,
Postponing love and the great anger,
For latter days when we are stronger.

But to go round and round again
In a dead dream of dead men,
From the stopped heart and the checked word;
This also has occurred,

And tall constructions from a first
Unquenched and undiminished thirst,
Out of weakness and much danger,
The laurel crown, the hero's posture.

To have suffered, though, to have done
With the black light of the first sun,
Though the drink's stale, the bread putrid,
This is beyond love and hatred;

To have worked out, to exceed
The Furies and the human need,
Is unpredictable, a grace
Of no time, no place.

The Mental Traveller

I travel'd thro' a Land of Men,
A Land of Men & Women too,
And heard & saw such dreadful things
As cold Earth wanderers never knew.

For there the Babe is born in joy
That was begotten in dire woe;
Just as we Reap in joy the fruit
Which we in bitter tears did sow.

And if the Babe is born a Boy
He's given to a Woman Old,
Who nails him down upon a rock,
Catches his shrieks in cups of gold.

She binds iron thorns around his head,
She pierces both his hands & feet,
She cuts his heart out at his side
To make it feel both cold & heat.

Her fingers number every Nerve,
Just as a Miser counts his gold;
She lives upon his shrieks & cries,
And she grows young as he grows old.

Till he becomes a bleeding youth,
And she becomes a Virgin bright;
Then he rends up his Manacles
And binds her down for his delight.

He plants himself in all her Nerves,
Just as a Husbandman his mould;
And she becomes his dwelling place
And Garden fruitful seventy fold.

An aged Shadow, soon he fades,
Wand'ring round an Earthly Cot,
Full filled all with gems & gold
Which he by industry had got.

And these are the gems of the Human Soul,
The rubies & pearls of a lovesick eye,
The countless gold of the akeing heart,
The martyr's groan & the lover's sigh.

They are his meat, they are his drink;
He feeds the Beggar & the Poor
And the wayfaring Traveller:
For ever open is his door.

His grief is their eternal joy;
They make the roofs & walls to ring;
Till from the fire on the hearth
A little Female Babe does spring.

And she is all of solid fire
And gems & gold, that none his hand
Dares stretch to touch her Baby form,
Or wrap her in his swaddling-band.

But She comes to the Man she loves,
If young or old, or rich or poor;
They soon drive out the aged Host,
A Beggar at another's door.

He wanders weeping far away,
Until some other take him in;
Oft blind & age-bent, sore distrest,
Until he can a Maiden win.

And to allay his freezing Age
The Poor Man takes her in his arms;
The Cottage fades before his sight,
The Garden & its lovely Charms.

The Guests are scatter'd thro' the land,
For the Eye altering alters all;
The Senses roll themselves in fear,
And the flat Earth becomes a Ball;

The stars, sun, Moon, all shrink away,
A desart vast without a bound,
And nothing left to eat or drink,
And a dark desart all around.

The honey of her Infant lips,
The bread & wine of her sweet smile,
The wild game of her roving Eye,
Does him to Infancy beguile;

For as he eats & drinks he grows
Younger & younger every day;
And on the desart wild they both
Wander in terror & dismay.

Like the wild Stag she flees away,
Her fear plants many a thicket wild;
While he pursues her night & day,
By various arts of Love beguil'd,

By various arts of Love & Hate,
Till the wide desart planted o'er
With Labyrinths of wayward Love,
Where roam the Lion, Wolf & Boar,

Till he becomes a wayward Babe,
And she a weeping Woman Old.
Then many a Lover wanders here;
The Sun & Stars are nearer roll'd.

The trees bring forth sweet Extacy
To all who in the desart roam;
Till many a City there is Built,
And many a pleasant Shepherd's home.

But when they find the frowning Babe,
Terror strikes thro' the region wide:
They cry 'The Babe! the Babe is Born!'
And flee away on Every side.

For who dare touch the frowning form,
His arm is wither'd to its root;
Lions, Boars, Wolves, all howling flee,
And every Tree does shed its fruit.

And none can touch that frowning form,
Except it be a Woman Old;
She nails him down upon the Rock,
And all is done as I have told.

ANNE BRADSTREET
1612-1672

To my Dear and Loving Husband

If ever two were one, then surely we.
If ever man were lov'd by wife, then thee;
If ever wife was happy in a man,
Compare with me ye women if you can.
I prize thy love more than whole Mines of gold,
Or all the riches that the East doth hold.
My love is such that Rivers cannot quench,
Nor ought but love from thee, give recompence.
Thy love is such I can no way repay,
The heavens reward thee manifold I pray.
Then while we live, in love lets so persever,
That when we live no more, we may live ever.

EMILY BRONTË
1818-1848

R. Alcona to J. Brenzaida

Cold in the earth and the deep snow piled above thee!
Far, far removed, cold in the dreary grave!
Have I forgot, my Only Love, to love thee,
Severed at last by Time's all-wearing wave?

Now, when alone, do my thoughts no longer hover
Over the mountains on Angora's shore;
Resting their wings where heath and fern-leaves cover
That noble heart for ever, ever more?

Cold in the earth, and fifteen wild Decembers
From those brown hills have melted into spring –
Faithful indeed is the spirit that remembers
After such years of change and suffering!

Sweet Love of youth, forgive if I forget thee
While the World's tide is bearing me along:
Sterner desires and darker hopes beset me,
Hopes which obscure but cannot do thee wrong.

No other Sun has lightened up my heaven;
No other Star has ever shone for me:
All my life's bliss from thy dear life was given –
All my life's bliss is in the grave with thee.

But when the days of golden dreams had perished
And even Despair was powerless to destroy,
Then did I learn how existence could be cherished,
Strengthened and fed without the aid of joy.

Then did I check the tears of useless passion,
Weaned my young soul from yearning after thine;
Sternly denied its burning wish to hasten
Down to that tomb already more than mine!

And even yet, I dare not let it languish,
Dare not indulge in Memory's rapturous pain:
Once drinking deep of that divinest anguish,
How could I seek the empty world again?

ROBERT BROWNING
1812-1889

Meeting At Night

i

The grey sea and the long black land;
And the yellow half-moon large and low;
And the startled little waves that leap
In fiery ringlets from their sleep,
As I gain the cove with pushing prow,
And quench its speed i' the slushy sand.

ii

Then a mile of warm sea-scented beach;
Three fields to cross till a farm appears;
A tap at the pane, the quick sharp scratch
And blue spurt of a lighted match,
And a voice less loud, thro' its joys and fears,
Than the two hearts beating each to each!

ROBERT BURNS
1759-1796

Song – For a' that and a' that –

Is there, for honest Poverty
    That hings his head, and a' that;
The coward-slave, we pass him by,
    We dare be poor for a' that!
  For a' that, and a' that,
    Our toils obscure, and a' that,
  The rank is but the guinea's stamp,
    The Man 's the gowd for a' that. –

What though on hamely fare we dine,
    Wear hoddin grey, and a' that.
Gie fools their silks, and knaves their wine,
    A Man 's a Man for a' that.
  For a' that, and a' that,
    Their tinsel show, and a' that;
  The honest man, though e'er sae poor,
    Is king o' men for a' that. –

Ye see yon birkie ca'd, a lord,
    Wha struts, and stares, and a' that,
Though hundreds worship at his word,
    He 's but a coof for a' that.
  For a' that, and a' that,
    His ribband, star and a' that,
  The man of independant mind,
    He looks and laughs at a' that. –

A prince can mak a belted knight,
 A marquis, duke, and a' that;
But an honest man' s aboon his might,
 Gude faith he mauna fa' that!
 For a' that, and a' that,
  Their dignities, and a' that,
 The pith o' Sense, and pride o' Worth,
  Are higher rank than a' that.–

Then let us pray that come it may,
 As come it will for a' that,
That Sense and Worth, o'er a' the earth
 Shall bear the gree, and a' that.
 For a' that, and a' that,
  It's comin yet, for a' that,
 That Man to Man the warld o'er,
  Shall brothers be for a' that.–

Darkness

I had a dream, which was not all a dream.
The bright sun was extinguish'd, and the stars
Did wander darkling in the eternal space,
Rayless, and pathless, and the icy earth
Swung blind and blackening in the moonless air;
Morn came and went – and came, and brought no day,
And men forgot their passions in the dread
Of this their desolation; and all hearts
Were chill'd into a selfish prayer for light:
And they did live by watchfires – and the thrones,
The palaces of crowned kings – the huts,
The habitations of all things which dwell,
Were burnt for beacons; cities were consumed,
And men were gather'd round their blazing homes
To look once more into each other's face;
Happy were those who dwelt within the eye
Of the volcanos, and their mountain-torch:
A fearful hope was all the world contain'd;
Forests were set on fire – but hour by hour
They fell and faded – and the crackling trunks
Extinguish'd with a crash – and all was black.
The brows of men by the despairing light
Wore an unearthly aspect, as by fits
The flashes fell upon them; some lay down
And hid their eyes and wept; and some did rest

Their chins upon their clenched hands, and smiled;
And others hurried to and fro, and fed
Their funeral piles with fuel, and look'd up
With mad disquietude on the dull sky,
The pall of a past world; and then again
With curses cast them down upon the dust,
And gnash'd their teeth and howl'd: the wild birds shriek'd
And, terrified, did flutter on the ground,
And flap their useless wings; the wildest brutes
Came tame and tremulous; and vipers crawl'd
And twined themselves among the multitude,
Hissing, but stingless – they were slain for food.
And War, which for a moment was no more,
Did glut himself again: – a meal was bought
With blood, and each sate sullenly apart
Gorging himself in gloom: no love was left;
All earth was but one thought – and that was death
Immediate and inglorious; and the pang
Of famine fed upon all entrails – men
Died, and their bones were tombless as their flesh;
The meagre by the meagre were devour'd,
Even dogs assail'd their masters, all save one,
And he was faithful to a corse, and kept
The birds and beasts and famish'd men at bay,
Till hunger clung them, or the dropping dead
Lured their lank jaws; himself sought out no food,
But with a piteous and perpetual moan,
And a quick desolate cry, licking the hand
Which answer'd not with a caress – he died.
The crowd was famish'd by degrees; but two
Of an enormous city did survive,

And they were enemies: they met beside
The dying embers of an altar-place
Where had been heap'd a mass of holy things
For an unholy usage; they raked up,
And shivering scraped with their cold skeleton hands
The feeble ashes, and their feeble breath
Blew for a little life, and made a flame
Which was a mockery; then they lifted up
Their eyes as it grew lighter, and beheld
Each other's aspects – saw, and shriek'd, and died –
Even of their mutual hideousness they died,
Unknowing who he was upon whose brow
Famine had written Fiend. The world was void,
The populous and the powerful was a lump,
Seasonless, herbless, treeless, manless, lifeless,
A lump of death – a chaos of hard clay.
The rivers, lakes, and ocean all stood still,
And nothing stirr'd within their silent depths;
Ships sailorless lay rotting on the sea,
And their masts fell down piecemeal: as they dropp'd
They slept on the abyss without a surge –
The waves were dead; the tides were in their grave,
The moon, their mistress, had expired before;
The winds were wither'd in the stagnant air,
And the clouds perish'd; Darkness had no need
Of aid from them – She was the Universe.

THOMAS CAMPION
1567–1620

There is a garden in her face

There is a garden in her face,
   Where roses and white lilies grow;
A heavenly paradise is that place,
   Wherein all pleasant fruits do flow.
There cherries grow which none may buy,
   Till 'Cherry-ripe' themselves do cry.

Those cherries fairly do enclose
   Of orient pearl a double row,
Which when her lovely laughter shows,
   They look like rosebuds filled with snow.
Yet them nor peer nor prince can buy,
   Till 'Cherry-ripe' themselves do cry.

Her eyes like angels watch them still;
   Her brows like bended bows do stand,
Threatening with piercing frowns to kill
   All that attempt with eye or hand
Those sacred cherries to come nigh,
   Till 'Cherry-ripe' themselves do cry.

THOMAS CAREW
1594-1640

The Second Rapture

No, worldling, no, 'tis not thy gold,
Which thou dost use but to behold;
Nor fortune, honour, nor long life,
Children, or friends, nor a good wife,
That makes thee happy: these things be
But shadows of felicity.
Give me a wench about thirteen,
Already voted to the queen
Of lust and lovers; whose soft hair,
Fann'd with the breath of gentle air,
O'erspreads her shoulders like a tent,
And is her veil and ornament;
Whose tender touch will make the blood
Wild in the aged and the good;
Whose kisses, fast'ned to the mouth
Of threescore years and longer slouth,
Renew the age; and whose bright eye
Obscures those lesser lights of sky;
Whose snowy breasts (if we may call
That snow, that never melts at all)
Makes Jove invent a new disguise,
In spite of Juno's jealousies;
Whose every part doth re-invite
The old decayed appetite;

And in whose sweet embraces I
May melt myself to lust, and die.
    This is true bliss, and I confess
    There is no other happiness.

LEWIS CARROLL
1832-1898

Jabberwocky

'Twas brillig, and the slithy toves
   Did gyre and gimble in the wabe:
All mimsy were the borogoves,
   And the mome raths outgrabe.

'Beware the Jabberwock, my son!
   The jaws that bite, the claws that catch!
Beware the Jubjub bird, and shun
   The frumious Bandersnatch!'

He took his vorpal sword in hand:
   Long time the manxome foe he sought –
So rested he by the Tumtum tree,
   And stood awhile in thought.

And, as in uffish thought he stood,
   The Jabberwock, with eyes of flame,
Came whiffling through the tulgey wood,
   And burbled as it came!

One, two! One, two! And through and through
   The vorpal blade went snicker-snack!
He left it dead, and with its head
   He went galumphing back.

'And hast thou slain the Jabberwock?
  Come to my arms, my beamish boy!
O frabjous day! Callooh! Callay!'
  He chortled in his joy.

'Twas brillig, and the slithy toves
  Did gyre and gimble in the wabe:
All mimsy were the borogoves,
  And the mome raths outgrabe.

JOHN CLARE
1793-1864

A Vision

I lost the love of heaven above,
   I spurned the lust of earth below,
I felt the sweets of fancied love,
   And hell itself my only foe.

I lost earth's joys, but felt the glow
   Of heaven's flame abound in me,
Till loveliness and I did grow
   The bard of immortality.

I loved, but woman fell away;
   I hid me from her faded fame.
I snatched the sun's eternal ray
   And wrote till earth was but a name.

In every language upon earth,
   On every shore, o'er every sea,
I gave my name immortal birth
   And kept my spirit with the free.

ARTHUR HUGH CLOUGH
1819-1861

The Latest Decalogue

Thou shalt have one God only; who
Would be at the expense of two?
No graven images may be
Worshipped, except the currency:
Swear not at all; for for thy curse
Thine enemy is none the worse:
At church on Sunday to attend
Will serve to keep the world thy friend:
Honour thy parents; that is, all
From whom advancement may befall:
Thou shalt not kill; but needst not strive
Officiously to keep alive:
Do not adultery commit;
Advantage rarely comes of it:
Thou shalt not steal; an empty feat,
When it's so lucrative to cheat:
Bear not false witness; let the lie
Have time on its own wings to fly:
Thou shalt not covet; but tradition
Approves all forms of competition.

The sum of all is, thou shalt love,
If any body, God above:
At any rate shall never labour
More than thyself to love thy neighbour.

SAMUEL TAYLOR COLERIDGE
1772-1834

Kubla Khan

In Xanadu did Kubla Khan
A stately pleasure-dome decree:
Where Alph, the sacred river, ran
Through caverns measureless to man
    Down to a sunless sea.
So twice five miles of fertile ground
With walls and towers were girdled round:
And there were gardens bright with sinuous rills,
Where blossomed many an incense-bearing tree;
And here were forests ancient as the hills,
Enfolding sunny spots of greenery.

But oh! that deep romantic chasm which slanted
Down the green hill athwart a cedarn cover!
A savage place! as holy and enchanted
As e'er beneath a waning moon was haunted
By woman wailing for her demon-lover!
And from this chasm, with ceaseless turmoil seething,
As if this earth in fast thick pants were breathing,
A mighty fountain momently was forced:
Amid whose swift half-intermitted burst
Huge fragments vaulted like rebounding hail,
Or chaffy grain beneath the thresher's flail:
And 'mid these dancing rocks at once and ever
It flung up momently the sacred river.

Five miles meandering with a mazy motion
Through wood and dale the sacred river ran,
Then reached the caverns measureless to man,
And sank in tumult to a lifeless ocean:
And 'mid this tumult Kubla heard from far
Ancestral voices prophesying war!
    The shadow of the dome of pleasure
    Floated midway on the waves;
    Where was heard the mingled measure
    From the fountain and the caves.
It was a miracle of rare device,
A sunny pleasure-dome with caves of ice!

    A damsel with a dulcimer
    In a vision once I saw:
    It was an Abyssinian maid,
    And on her dulcimer she play'd,
    Singing of Mount Abora.
    Could I revive within me
    Her symphony and song,
    To such a deep delight 'twould win me,
That with music loud and long,
I would build that dome in air,
That sunny dome! those caves of ice!
And all who heard should see them there,
And all should cry, Beware! Beware!
His flashing eyes, his floating hair!
Weave a circle round him thrice,
And close your eyes with holy dread,
For he on honey-dew hath fed,
And drunk the milk of Paradise.

CHARLES COTTON
1630-1687

An Epitaph on M.H.

In this cold monument lies one,
That I knew who has lain upon,
The happier He: her sight would charm,
And touch have kept King David warm.
Lovely, as is the dawning East,
Was this marble's frozen guest;
As soft, and snowy, as that down
Adorns the blow-ball's frizzled crown;
As straight and slender as the crest,
Or antlet of the one-beam'd beast;
Pleasant as th' odorous month of May:
As glorious, and as light as day.

Whom I admir'd, as soon as knew,
And now her memory pursue
With such a superstitious lust,
That I could fumble with her dust.

She all perfections had, and more,
Tempting, as if design'd a whore,
For so she was; and since there are
Such, I could wish them all as fair.

Pretty she was, and young, and wise,
And in her calling so precise,
That industry had made her prove
The sucking school-mistress of love:
And Death, ambitious to become
Her pupil, left his ghastly home,
And, seeing how we us'd her here,
The raw-boned rascal ravish'd her.

Who, pretty soul, resign'd her breath,
To seek new lechery in Death.

The Innocent Ill

Though all thy gestures and discourses be
    Coyn'd and stamp'd by *Modesty*,
    Though from thy *Tongue* ne're slipt away
One word which *Nuns* at th' *Altar* might not say,
    Yet such a sweetness, such a grace
    In all thy *speech* appear,
    That what to th' *Eye* a beauteous *face*,
    That thy *Tongue* is to th' *Ear*.
  So cunningly it wounds the heart,
  It strikes such heat through every part,
That thou a *Tempter* worse than *Satan* art.

Though in thy thoughts scarce any Tracks have bin
    So much as of *Original* Sin,
    Such charms thy *Beauty* wears as might
Desires in dying confest *Saints* excite.
    Thou with strange *Adultery*
    Dost in each breast a *Brothel keep*;
    Awake all men do lust for thee,
    And some *enjoy* Thee when they *sleep*.
  Ne're before did *Woman* live,
  Who to such *Multitudes* did give
The *Root* and *cause* of *Sin*, but only *Eve*.

Though in thy breast so quick a *Pity* be,
    That a *Flies Death's* a *wound* to thee.
    Though savage, and rock-hearted those
Appear, that weep not ev'en *Romances* woes.
    Yet ne're before was *Tyrant* known,
    Whose rage was of so large extent,
    The ills thou dost are *whole* thine own,
    Thou'rt *Principal* and *Instrument*,
  In all the deaths that come from you,
  You do the *treble Office* do
Of *Judge*, of *Tort'urer*, and of *Weapon* too.

Thou *lovely Instrument* of *angry Fate*,
    Which *God* did for our faults create!
    Thou *Pleasant, Universal Ill*,
Which *sweet* as *Health*, yet like a *Plague* dost *kill*!
    Thou kind, well-natur'ed *Tyranny*!
    Thou *Chaste* committer of a *Rape*!
    Thou *voluntary Destiny*,
    Which no man *Can*, or *Would* escape!
  So gentle, and so glad to spare,
  So wondrous good, and wondrous fair,
(We know) e'ven the *Destroying Angels* are.

WILLIAM COWPER
1731-1800

Lines Written During a Period of Insanity

Hatred and vengeance, my eternal portion,
Scarce can endure delay of execution,
Wait, with impatient readiness, to seize my
                       Soul in a moment.

Damn'd below Judas: more abhorr'd than he was,
Who for a few pence sold his holy Master.
Twice betrayed Jesus me, the last delinquent,
                       Deems the profanest.

Man disavows, and Deity disowns me:
Hell might afford my miseries a shelter;
Therefore hell keeps her ever hungry mouths all
                       Bolted against me.

Hard lot! encompass'd with a thousand dangers;
Weary, faint, trembling with a thousand terrors;
I'm called, if vanquish'd, to receive a sentence
                       Worse than Abiram's.

Him the vindictive rod of angry justice
Sent quick and howling to the centre headlong;
I, fed with judgment, in a fleshly tomb, am
                       Buried above ground.

e.e. cummings
1894-1962

next to of course god america i

'next to of course god america i
love you land of the pilgrims' and so forth oh
say can you see by the dawn's early my
country 'tis of centuries come and go
and are no more what of it we should worry
in every language even deafanddumb
thy sons acclaim your glorious name by gorry
by jingo by gee by gosh by gum
why talk of beauty what could be more beaut-
iful than these heroic happy dead
who rushed like lions to the roaring slaughter
they did not stop to think they died instead
then shall the voice of liberty be mute?'

He spoke. And drank rapidly a glass of water

Love is a sickness full of woes

Love is a sickness full of woes,
All remedies refusing;
A plant that with most cutting grows,
Most barren with best using.
                    Why so?
More we enjoy it, more it dies;
If not enjoyed, it sighing cries,
                    Hey ho.
Love is a torment of the mind,
A tempest everlasting;
And Jove hath made it of a kind,
Not well, nor full nor fasting.
                    Why so?
More we enjoy it, more it dies;
If not enjoyed, it sighing cries,
                    Hey ho.

On a Pair of Garters

Go, loving woodbine, clip with lovely grace
Those two sweet plants which bear the flowers of love;
Go, silken vines, those tender elms embrace
Which flourish still although their roots do move.
As soon as you possess your blessed places
You are advancèd and ennobled more
Than diadems, which were white silken laces
That ancient kings about their forehead wore.
Sweet bands, take heed lest you ungently bind,
Or with your strictness make too deep a print:
Was never tree had such a tender rind,
Although her inward heart be hard as flint.
And let your knots be fast and loose at will:
She must be free, though I stand bounden still.

There came a Wind like a Bugle

There came a Wind like a Bugle –
It quivered through the Grass
And a Green Chill upon the Heat
So ominous did pass
We barred the Windows and the Doors
As from an Emerald Ghost –
The Doom's electric Moccasin
That very instant passed –
On a strange Mob of panting Trees
And Fences fled away
And Rivers where the Houses ran
Those looked that lived – that Day –
The Bell within the steeple wild
The flying tidings told –
How much can come
And much can go,
And yet abide the World!

JOHN DONNE
1572-1631

Twicknam Garden

Blasted with sighs, and surrounded with teares,
   Hither I come to seeke the spring,
   And at mine eyes, and at mine eares,
Receive such balmes, as else cure every thing;
   But O, selfe traytor, I do bring
The spider love, which transubstantiates all,
   And can convert Manna to gall,
And that this place may thoroughly be thought
   True Paradise, I have the serpent brought.

'Twere wholsomer for mee, that winter did
   Benight the glory of this place,
   And that a grave frost did forbid
These trees to laugh, and mocke mee to my face;
   But that I may not this disgrace
Indure, nor yet leave loving, Love let mee
   Some senslesse peece of this place bee;
Make me a mandrake, so I may groane here,
   Or a stone fountaine weeping out my yeare.

Hither with christall vyals, lovers come,
    And take my teares, which are loves wine,
    And try your mistresse Teares at home,
For all are false, that tast not just like mine;
    Alas, hearts do not in eyes shine,
Nor can you more judge womans thoughts by teares,
    Than by her shadow, what she weares.
O perverse sexe, where none is true but shee,
    Who's therefore true, because her truth kills mee.

ERNEST DOWSON
1867-1900

Non Sum Qualis Eram Bonae
Sub Regno Cynarae

Last night, ah, yesternight, betwixt her lips and mine
There fell thy shadow, Cynara! thy breath was shed
Upon my soul between the kisses and the wine;
And I was desolate and sick of an old passion,
　　Yea, I was desolate and bowed my head:
I have been faithful to thee, Cynara! in my fashion.

All night upon mine heart I felt her warm heart beat,
Night-long within mine arms in love and sleep she lay;
Surely the kisses of her bought red mouth were sweet;
But I was desolate and sick of an old passion,
　　When I awoke and found the dawn was gray:
I have been faithful to thee, Cynara! in my fashion.

I have forgot much, Cynara! gone with the wind,
Flung roses, roses riotously with the throng,
Dancing, to put thy pale, lost lilies out of mind;
But I was desolate and sick of an old passion,
　　Yea, all the time, because the dance was long:
I have been faithful to thee, Cynara! in my fashion.

I cried for madder music and for stronger wine,
But when the feast is finished and the lamps expire,
Then falls thy shadow, Cynara! the night is thine;
And I am desolate and sick of an old passion,
     Yea hungry for the lips of my desire:
I have been faithful to thee, Cynara! in my fashion.

MICHAEL DRAYTON
1563-1631

Since there's no help, come let us kiss and part

Since there's no help, come let us kiss and part.
Nay, I have done; you get no more of me,
And I am glad, yea glad with all my heart,
That thus so cleanly I myself can free;
Shake hands for ever, cancel all our vows,
And when we meet at any time again,
Be it not seen in either of our brows
That we one jot of former love retain.
Now at the last gasp of Love's latest breath,
When his pulse failing, passion speechless lies,
When faith is kneeling by his bed of death,
And innocence is closing up his eyes,
    Now if thou wouldst, when all have given him over,
    From death to life, thou mightst him yet recover.

A Song for St. Cecilia's Day
November 22, 1687

I

From Harmony, from heav'nly Harmony
  This universal Frame began;
 When Nature underneath a heap
  Of jarring Atoms lay,
 And cou'd not heave her Head,
The tuneful Voice was heard from high,
  Arise, ye more than dead.
Then cold and hot and moist and dry
 In order to their Stations leap,
  And MUSICK'S pow'r obey.
From Harmony, from heavenly Harmony
  This universal Frame began:
  From Harmony to Harmony
Through all the Compass of the Notes it ran,
The Diapason closing full in Man.

2

What Passion cannot MUSICK raise and quell?
  When *Jubal* struck the corded Shell,
 His listening Brethren stood around,
  And, wond'ring, on their Faces fell
 To worship that Celestial Sound:

Less than a God they thought there could not dwell
    Within the hollow of that Shell,
    That spoke so sweetly, and so well.
What Passion cannot MUSICK raise and quell?

3

    The TRUMPETS loud Clangor
      Excites us to Arms
    With shrill Notes of Anger
      And mortal Alarms.
    The double double double beat
      Of the thund'ring DRUM
      Cries, hark the Foes come;
Charge, Charge, 'tis too late to retreat.

4

    The soft complaining FLUTE
    In dying Notes discovers
    The Woes of hopeless Lovers,
Whose Dirge is whisper'd by the warbling LUTE.

5

    Sharp VIOLINS proclaim
Their jealous Pangs and Desperation,
Fury, frantic Indignation,
Depths of Pains and Height of Passion,
    For the fair, disdainful Dame.

6

But oh! what Art can teach
What human Voice can reach
    The sacred ORGANS Praise?
Notes inspiring holy Love,
Notes that wing their heavenly Ways
    To mend the Choirs above.

7

Orpheus cou'd lead the savage race,
And Trees unrooted left their Place,
    Sequacious of the Lyre;
But bright CECILIA rais'd the Wonder high'r:
When to her Organ vocal Breath was given,
An Angel heard, and straight appear'd
    Mistaking Earth for Heav'n.

Grand Chorus
As from the Pow'r of Sacred Lays
*   The Spheres began to move,*
And sung the great Creator's Praise
*   To all the bless'd above;*
So, when the last and dreadful Hour
This crumbling Pageant shall devour,
The TRUMPET shall be heard on high,
The dead shall live, the living die,
And MUSICK shall untune the Sky.

SIR EDWARD DYER
1543-1607

The lowest trees have tops, the ant her gall

The lowest trees have tops, the ant her gall,
The fly her spleen, the little spark his heat:
The slender hairs cast shadows, though but small,
And bees have stings, although they be not great;
   Seas have their source, and so have shallow springs;
   And love is love, in beggars and in kings.

Where waters smoothest run, there deepest are the fords,
The dial stirs, yet none perceives it move;
The firmest faith is found in fewest words,
The turtles do not sing, and yet they love;
   True hearts have ears and eyes, no tongues to speak;
   They hear and see, and sigh, and then they break.

T. S. ELIOT
1888-1965

La Figlia Che Piange
O quam te memorem virgo . . .

Stand on the highest pavement of the stair –
Lean on a garden urn –
Weave, weave the sunlight in your hair –
Clasp your flowers to you with a pained surprise –
Fling them to the ground and turn
With a fugitive resentment in your eyes:
But weave, weave the sunlight in your hair.

So I would have had him leave,
So I would have had her stand and grieve,
So he would have left
As the soul leaves the body torn and bruised,
As the mind deserts the body it has used.
I should find
Some way incomparably light and deft,
Some way we both should understand,
Simple and faithless as a smile and shake of the hand.

She turned away, but with the autumn weather
Compelled my imagination many days,
Many days and many hours:
Her hair over her arms and her arms full of flowers.
And I wonder how they should have been together!
I should have lost a gesture and a pose.
Sometimes these cogitations still amaze
The troubled midnight and the noon's repose.

WILLIAM EMPSON
1906-1984

Let it go

It is this deep blankness is the real thing strange.
   The more things happen to you the more you can't
      Tell or remember even what they were.

The contradictions cover such a range.
   The talk would talk and go so far aslant.
      You don't want madhouse and the whole thing there.

ROBERT FROST
1874-1963

Provide, Provide

The witch that came (the withered hag)
To wash the steps with pail and rag,
Was once the beauty Abishag,

The picture pride of Hollywood.
Too many fall from great and good
For you to doubt the likelihood.

Die early and avoid the fate.
Or if predestined to die late,
Make up your mind to die in state.

Make the whole stock exchange your own!
If need be occupy a throne,
Where nobody can call *you* crone.

Some have relied on what they knew;
Others on being simply true.
What worked for them might work for you.

No memory of having starred
Atones for later disregard,
Or keeps the end from being hard.

Better to go down dignified
With boughten friendship at your side
Than none at all. Provide, provide!

The Green Knight's Farewell to Fancy

Fancy (quoth he) *farewell*, whose badge I long did bear,
And in my hat full harebrainedly, thy flowers did I wear:
Too late I find (at last), thy fruits are nothing worth,
Thy blossoms fall and fade full fast, though bravery bring
                                 them forth.
By thee I hoped always, in deep delights to dwell,
But since I find thy fickleness, *Fancy* (quoth he) *farewell*.

Thou mad'st me live in love, which wisdom bids me hate,
Thou bleared'st mine eyes and mad'st me think, that faith
                               was mine by fate:
By thee those bitter sweets, did please my taste alway,
By thee I thought that love was light, and pain was but a
                               play:
I thought that beauty's blaze, was meet to bear the bell,
And since I find myself deceived, *Fancy* (quoth he) *farewell*.

The gloss of gorgeous courts, by thee did please mine eye,
A stately sight me thought it was, to see the brave go by:
To see their feathers flaunt, to mark their strange device,
To lie along in ladies' laps, to lisp and make it nice:
To fawn and flatter both, I liked sometime well,
But since I see how vain it is, *Fancy* (quoth he) *farewell*.

When court had cast me off, I toiled at the plough
My fancy stood in strange conceits, to thrive I wot not
                                                    how:
By mills, by making malt, by sheep and eke by swine,
By duck and drake, by pig and goose, by calves and keeping
                                                    kine:
By feeding bullocks fat, when price at markets fell,
But since my swains eat up the gains, *Fancy* (quoth he)
                                                    farewell.

In hunting of the deer, my fancy took delight,
All forests knew, my folly still, the moonshine was my
                                                    light:
In frosts I felt no cold, a sunburnt hue was best,
I sweat and was in temper still, my watching seemed rest:
What dangers deep I passed, it folly were to tell,
And since I sigh to think thereon, *Fancy* (quoth he) *farewell.*

A fancy fed me once, to write in verse and rhyme,
To wray my grief, to crave reward, to cover still my crime:
To frame a long discourse, on stirring of a straw,
To rumble rhyme in raff and ruff, yet all not worth a haw:
To hear it said there goeth, the *man that writes so well,*
But since I see, what poets be, *Fancy* (quoth he) *farewell.*

At music's sacred sound, my fancies eft begun,
In concords, discords, notes and clefs, in tunes of unison:
In *Hierarchies* and strains, in rests, in rule and space,
In monochords and moving modes, in *Burdens* underbass:
In descants and in chants, I strained many a yell,
But since musicians be so mad, *Fancy* (quoth he) *farewell.*

To plant strange country fruits, to sow such seeds likewise,
To dig and delve for new found roots, where old might
well suffice:
To prune the water boughs, to pick the mossy trees,
(Oh how it pleased my fancy once) to kneel upon my knees,
To griff a pippin stock, when sap begins to swell:
But since the gains scarce quit the cost, *Fancy* (quoth he)
farewell.

Fancy (quoth he) *farewell*, which made me follow drums,
Where powdered bullets serves for sauce, to every dish that
comes,
Where treason lurks in trust, where *Hope* all hearts beguiles,
Where mischief lieth still in wait, when fortune friendly
smiles:
Where one day's prison proves, that all such heavens are
hell,
And such I feel the fruits thereof, *Fancy* (quoth he) *farewell.*

If reason rule my thoughts, and God vouchsafe me grace,
Then comfort of philosophy, shall make me change my
race,
And fond I shall it find, that Fancy sets to show,
For weakly stands that building still, which lacketh grace by
low:
But since I must accept, my fortunes as they fell,
I say God send me better speed, and *Fancy now farewell.*

BARNABE GOOGE
1540-1594

The oftener seen, the more I lust

The oftener seen, the more I lust,
The more I lust, the more I smart,
The more I smart, the more I trust,
The more I trust, the heavier heart,
The heavy heart breeds mine unrest;
Thy absence therefore like I best.

The rarer seen, the less in mind,
The less in mind, the lesser pain,
The lesser pain, less grief I find,
The lesser grief, the greater gain,
The greater gain, the merrier I;
Therefore I wish thy sight to fly.

The further off, the more I joy,
The more I joy, the happier life,
The happier life, less hurts annoy,
The lesser hurts, pleasure most rife;
Such pleasures rife shall I obtain
When distance doth depart us twain.

W. S. GRAHAM
1918–1986

I leave this at your ear
For Nessie Dunsmuir

I leave this at your ear for when you wake,
A creature in its abstract cage asleep.
Your dreams blindfold you by the light they make.

The owl called from the naked–woman tree
As I came down by the Kyle farm to hear
Your house silent by the speaking sea.

I have come late but I have come before
Later with slaked steps from stone to stone
To hope to find you listening for the door.

I stand in the ticking room. My dear, I take
A moth kiss from your breath. The shore gulls cry.
I leave this at your ear for when you wake.

ROBERT GRAVES
1895-1986

The White Goddess

All saints revile her, and all sober men
Ruled by the God Apollo's golden mean –
In scorn of which we sailed to find her
In distant regions likeliest to hold her
Whom we desired above all things to know,
Sister of the mirage and echo.

It was a virtue not to stay,
To go our headstrong and heroic way
Seeking her out at the volcano's head,
Among pack ice, or where the track had faded
Beyond the cavern of the seven sleepers:
Whose broad high brow was white as any leper's,
Whose eyes were blue, with rowan-berry lips,
With hair curled honey-coloured to white hips.

Green sap of Spring in the young wood a-stir
Will celebrate the Mountain Mother,
And every song-bird shout awhile for her;
But we are gifted, even in November
Rawest of seasons, with so huge a sense
Of her nakedly worn magnificence
We forget cruelty and past betrayal,
Heedless of where the next bright bolt may fall.

THOMAS GRAY
1716-1771

On Lord Holland's Seat Near Margate, Kent

Old and abandoned by each venal friend,
　　Here Holland took the pious resolution
To smuggle some few years and strive to mend
　　A broken character and constitution.
On this congenial spot he fixed his choice;
　　Earl Godwin trembled for his neighbouring sand;
Here sea-gulls scream and cormorants rejoice,
　　And mariners, though shipwrecked, dread to land.
Here reign the blustering North and blighting East,
　　No tree is heard to whisper, bird to sing:
Yet nature cannot furnish out the feast,
　　Art he invokes new horrors still to bring.
Now mouldering fanes and battlements arise,
　　Arches and turrets nodding to their fall,
Unpeopled palaces delude his eyes,
　　And mimic desolation covers all.
'Ah', said the sighing peer, 'had Bute been true
　　Nor Shelburne's, Rigby's, Calcraft's friendship vain,
Far other scenes than these had blessed our view
　　And realised the ruins that we feign.
Purged by the sword and beautified by fire,
　　Then had we seen proud London's hated walls:
Owls might have hooted in St Peter's choir,
　　And foxes stunk and littered in St Paul's.'

68

FULKE GREVILLE, LORD BROOKE
1554-1628

Love, the delight of all well-thinking minds

Love, the delight of all well-thinking minds;
Delight, the fruit of virtue dearly lov'd;
Virtue, the highest good, that reason finds;
Reason, the fire wherein men's thoughts be prov'd;
   Are from the world by Nature's power bereft,
   And in one creature, for her glory, left.

Beauty, her cover is, the eyes' true pleasure;
In honour's fame she lives, the ears' sweet music;
Excess of wonder grows from her true measure;
Her worth is passion's wound, and passion's physic;
   From her true heart, clear springs of wisdom flow,
   Which imag'd in her words and deeds, men know.

Time fain would stay, that she might never leave her,
Place doth rejoice, that she must needs contain her,
Death craves of Heaven, that she may not bereave her,
The Heavens know their own, and do maintain her;
   Delight, love, reason, virtue let it be,
   To set all women light, but only she.

JOHN HALL
1627-1656

On an Hour-Glass

My Life is measur'd by this glass, this glass
By all those little Sands that thorough pass.
See how they press, see how they strive, which shall
With greatest speed and greatest quickness fall.
See how they raise a little Mount, and then
With their own weight do level it again.
But when th'have all got thorough, they give o're
Their nimble sliding down, and move no more.
Just such is man whose hours still forward run,
Being almost finished ere they are begun;
So perfect nothings, such light blasts are we,
That ere w'are aught at all, we cease to be.
Do what we will, our hasty minutes fly,
And while we sleep, what do we else but die?
How transient are our Joys, how short their day!
They creep on towards us, but fly away.
How stinging are our sorrows! where they gain
But the least footing, there they will remain.
How groundless are our hopes, how they deceive
Our childish thoughts, and only sorrow leave!
How real are our fears! they blast us still,
Still rend us, still with gnawing passions fill;
How senseless are our wishes, yet how great!
With what toil we pursue them, with what sweat!

Yet most times for our hurts, so small we see,
Like Children crying for some Mercury.
This gapes for Marriage, yet his fickle head
Knows not what cares wait on a Marriage bed.
This vows Virginity, yet knows not what
Loneness, grief, discontent, attends that state.
Desires of wealth another's wishes hold,
And yet how many have been chok'd with Gold?
This only hunts for honour, yet who shall
Ascend the higher, shall more wretched fall.
This thirsts for knowledge, yet how is it bought
With many a sleepless night and racking thought?
This needs will travel, yet how dangers lay
Most secret Ambuscado's in the way?
These triumph in their Beauty, though it shall
Like a pluck'd Rose or fading Lily fall.
Another boasts strong arms, 'las Giants have
By silly Dwarfs been dragg'd unto their grave.
These ruffle in rich silk, though ne'er so gay,
A well plum'd Peacock is more gay than they.
Poor man, what art! A Tennis ball of Error,
A Ship of Glass, toss'd in a Sea of terror,
Issuing in blood and sorrow from the womb,
Crawling in tears and mourning to the tomb,
How slippery are thy paths, how sure thy fall,
How art thou Nothing when th'art most of all!

THOMAS HARDY
1840-1928

An Upbraiding

Now I am dead you sing to me
    The songs we used to know,
But while I lived you had no wish
    Or care for doing so.

Now I am dead you come to me
    In the moonlight, comfortless;
Ah, what would I have given alive
    To win such tenderness!

When you are dead, and stand to me
    Not differenced, as now,
But like again, will you be cold
    As when we lived, or how?

W. E. HENLEY
1849-1903

Madam Life's a piece in bloom

Madam Life's a piece in bloom
   Death goes dogging everywhere:
She's the tenant of the room,
   He's the ruffian on the stair.

You shall see her as a friend,
   You shall bilk him once or twice;
But he'll trap you in the end,
   And he'll stick you for her price.

With his kneebones at your chest,
   And his knuckles in your throat,
You would reason – plead – protest!
   Clutching at her petticoat;

But she's heard it all before,
   Well she knows you've had your fun,
Gingerly she gains the door,
   And your little job is done.

EDWARD,
LORD HERBERT OF CHERBURY
1583-1648

A Description

I sing her worth and praises high,
Of whom a poet cannot lie.
The little world the great shall blaze:
Sea, earth her body; heaven her face;
Her hair sunbeams, whose every part
Lightens, inflames each lover's heart,
That thus you prove the axiom true,
Whilst the sun help'd nature in you.

Her front the white and azure sky,
In light and glory raised high;
Being o'ercast by a cloudy frown,
All hearts and eyes dejecteth down.

Her each brow a celestial bow,
Which through this sky her light doth show,
Which doubled, if it strange appear,
The sun's likewise is doubled there.

Her either cheek a blushing morn,
Which, on the wings of beauty borne,
Doth never set, but only fair
Shineth, exalted in her hair.

Within her mouth, heaven's heav'n, reside
Her words: the soul's there glorifi'd.

Her nose th' equator of this globe,
Where nakedness, beauty's best robe,
Presents a form all hearts to win.

74

Last Nature made that dainty chin,
Which, that it might in every fashion
Answer the rest, a constellation,
Like to a desk, she there did place
To write the wonders of her face.

In this celestial frontispiece,
Where happiness eternal lies,
First arranged stand three senses,
This heaven's intelligences,
Whose several motions, sweet combin'd,
Come from the first mover, her mind.

The weight of this harmonic sphere
The Atlas of her neck doth bear,
Whose favours day to us imparts,
When frowns make night in lovers' hearts.

Two foaming billows are her breasts,
That carry rais'd upon their crests
The Tyrian fish: more white's their foam
Than that whence Venus once did come.

Here take her by the hand, my Muse,
With that sweet foe to make my truce,
To compact manna best compar'd,
Whose dewy inside's not full hard.

Her waist's an invers'd pyramis,
Upon whose cone love's trophy is.

Her belly is that magazine
At whose peep Nature did resign
That precious mould by which alone
There can be framed such a one.

At th' entrance of which hidden treasure,
Happy making above measure,
Two alabaster pillars stand,

To warn all passage from that land;
At foot whereof engraved is
The sad *Non ultra* of man's bliss.
  The back of this most precious frame
Holds up in majesty the same,
Where, to make music to all hearts,
Love bound the descant of her parts.
  Though all this Beauty's temple be,
There's known within no deity
Save virtues shrin'd within her will.
As I began, so say I still,
I sing her worth and praises high,
Of whom a poet cannot lie.

Love

Love bade me welcome: yet my soul drew back,
            Guilty of dust and sin.
But quick-ey'd Love, observing me grow slack
            From my first entrance in,
Drew nearer to me, sweetly questioning,
            If I lack'd any thing.

A guest, I answer'd, worthy to be here:
            Love said, You shall be he.
I the unkind, ungrateful? Ah my dear,
            I cannot look on thee.
Love took my hand, and smiling did reply,
            Who made the eyes but I?

Truth Lord, but I have marr'd them: let my shame
            Go where it doth deserve.
And know you not, says Love, who bore the blame?
            My dear, then I will serve.
You must sit down, says Love, and taste my meat:
            So I did sit and eat.

ROBERT HERRICK
1591-1674

Whenas in silks my Julia goes

Whenas in silks my Julia goes,
Then, then, methinks, how sweetly flows
The liquefaction of her clothes.

Next, when I cast mine eyes and see
That brave vibration each way free;
O how that glittering taketh me!

GERARD MANLEY HOPKINS
1844-1889

No worst, there is none. Pitched past pitch of grief

No worst, there is none. Pitched past pitch of grief,
More pangs will, schooled at forepangs, wilder wring.
Comforter, where, where is your comforting?
Mary, mother of us, where is your relief?
My cries heave, herds-long; huddle in a main, a chief
Woe, wórld-sorrow; on an áge-old anvil wince and sing –
Then lull, then leave off. Fury had shrieked 'No ling-
ering! Let me be fell: force I must be brief.'

O the mind, mind has mountains; cliffs of fall
Frightful, sheer, no-man-fathomed. Hold them cheap
May who ne'er hung there. Nor does long our small
Durance deal with that steep or deep. Here! creep,
Wretch, under a comfort serves in a whirlwind: all
Life death does end and each day dies with sleep.

Absence, hear my protestation

Absence, hear my protestation
    Against thy strength
    Distance and length,
Do what thou canst for alteration:
    For hearts of truest metal
    Absence doth join, and Time doth settle.

Who loves a mistress of right quality,
    His mind hath found
    Affection's ground
Beyond time, place, and all mortality:
    To hearts that cannot vary
    Absence is present, Time doth tarry.

My senses want their outward motion
    Which now within
    Reason doth win,
Redoubled by her secret notion;
    Like rich men that take pleasure
    In hiding more than handling treasure.

By absence this good means I gain,
    That I can catch her
    (Where none can watch her)
In some close corner of my brain:
    There I embrace and kiss her,
    And so enjoy her, and none miss her.

A. E. HOUSMAN
1859-1936

Her strong enchantments failing

Her strong enchantments failing,
    Her towers of fear in wreck,
Her limbecks dried of poisons
    And the knife at her neck,

The Queen of air and darkness
    Begins to shrill and cry,
'O young man, O my slayer,
    To-morrow you shall die.'

O Queen of air and darkness,
    I think 'tis truth you say,
And I shall die to-morrow;
    But you will die to-day.

Her Triumph

See the Chariot at hand here of Love,
  Wherein my Lady rideth!
Each that draws is a swan or a dove,
  And well the car Love guideth.
As she goes, all hearts do duty
      Unto her beauty;
And enamour'd do wish, so they might
      But enjoy such a sight,
That they still were to run by her side,
Thorough swords, thorough seas, whither she would ride.

Do but look on her eyes, they do light
  All that Love's world compriseth!
Do but look on her hair, it is bright
  As Love's star when it riseth!
Do but mark, her forehead's smoother
      Than words that soothe her;
And from her arch'd brows such a grace
      Sheds itself through the face,
As alone there triumphs to the life
All the gain, all the good, of the elements' strife.

Have you seen but a bright lily grow
    Before rude hands have touch'd it?
Have you mark'd but the fall of the snow
    Before the soil hath smutch'd it?
Have you felt the wool of the beaver,
        Or swan's down ever?
Or have smelt of the bud of the brier,
        Or the nard in the fire?
Or have tasted the bag of the bee?
O so white, O so soft, O so sweet is she!

JAMES JOYCE

Ecce Puer

Of the dark past
A child is born;
With joy and grief
My heart is torn.

Calm in his cradle
The living lies.
May love and mercy
Unclose his eyes!

Young life is breathed
On the glass;
The world that was not
Comes to pass.

A child is sleeping:
An old man gone.
O, father forsaken,
Forgive your son!

JOHN KEATS
1795-1821

Ode to a Nightingale

My heart aches, and a drowsy numbness pains
   My sense, as though of hemlock I had drunk,
Or emptied some dull opiate to the drains
   One minute past, and Lethe-wards had sunk:
'Tis not through envy of thy happy lot,
   But being too happy in thy happiness, –
      That thou, light-wingèd Dryad of the trees,
      In some melodious plot
   Of beechen green, and shadows numberless,
   Singest of summer in full-throated ease.

O for a draught of vintage, that hath been
   Cool'd a long age in the deep-delvèd earth,
Tasting of Flora and the country-green,
   Dance, and Provencal song, and sunburnt mirth!
O for a beaker full of the warm South,
   Full of the true, the blushful Hippocrene,
      With beaded bubbles winking at the brim,
      And purple-stainèd mouth;
   That I might drink and leave the world unseen,
   And with thee fade away into the forest dim:

Fade far away, dissolve, and quite forget
  What thou amongst the leaves hast never known,
The weariness, the fever, and the fret
  Here, where men sit and hear each other groan;
Where palsy shakes a few, sad, last grey hairs,
  Where youth grows pale, and spectre-thin, and dies;
    Where but to think is to be full of sorrow
      And leaden-eyed despairs;
    Where Beauty cannot keep her lustrous eyes,
      Or new Love pine at them beyond to-morrow.

Away! away! for I will fly to thee,
  Not charioted by Bacchus and his pards,
But on the viewless wings of Poesy,
  Though the dull brain perplexes and retards:
Already with thee! tender is the night,
  And haply the Queen-Moon is on her throne,
    Cluster'd around by all her starry Fays;
      But here there is no light,
    Save what from heaven is with the breezes blown
      Through verdurous glooms and winding mossy ways.

I cannot see what flowers are at my feet,
  Nor what soft incense hangs upon the boughs,
But, in embalmèd darkness, guess each sweet
  Wherewith the seasonable month endows
The grass, the thicket, and the fruit-tree wild;
  White hawthorn, and the pastoral eglantine;
    Fast-fading violets cover'd up in leaves;
      And mid-May's eldest child,
    The coming musk-rose, full of dewy wine,
      The murmurous haunt of flies on summer eves.

Darkling I listen; and for many a time
I have been half in love with easeful Death,
Call'd him soft names in many a musèd rhyme,
To take into the air my quiet breath;
Now more than ever seems it rich to die,
To cease upon the midnight with no pain,
While thou art pouring forth thy soul abroad
In such an ecstasy!
Still wouldst thou sing, and I have ears in vain –
To thy high requiem become a sod.

Thou wast not born for death, immortal Bird!
No hungry generations tread thee down;
The voice I hear this passing night was heard
In ancient days by emperor and clown:
Perhaps the self-same song that found a path
Through the sad heart of Ruth, when sick for home,
She stood in tears amid the alien corn;
The same that oft-times hath
Charm'd magic casements, opening on the foam
Of perilous seas, in faery lands forlorn.

Forlorn! the very word is like a bell
To toll me back from thee to my sole self.
Adieu! the fancy cannot cheat so well
As she is famed to do, deceiving elf,
Adieu! adieu! thy plaintive anthem fades
Past the near meadows, over the still stream,
Up the hill-side, and now 'tis buried deep
In the next valley-glades:
Was it a vision, or a waking dream?
Fled is that music: – do I wake or sleep?

RUDYARD KIPLING
1865-1936

The Gods of the Copybook Headings

As I pass through my incarnations in every age and
    race,
I make my proper prostrations to the Gods of the Market-
    Place.
Peering through reverent fingers I watch them flourish and
    fall,
And the Gods of the Copybook Headings, I notice, outlast
    them all.

We were living in trees when they met us. They showed us
    each in turn
That Water would certainly wet us, as Fire would certainly
    burn:
But we found them lacking in Uplift, Vision and Breadth
    of Mind,
So we left them to teach the Gorillas while we followed
    The March of Mankind.

We moved as the Spirit listed. *They* never altered their
    pace,
Being neither cloud nor wind-borne like the Gods of the
    Market-Place;
But they always caught up with our progress, and presently
    word would come
That a tribe had been wiped off its icefield, or the lights
    had gone out in Rome.

With the Hopes that our World is built on they were
  utterly out of touch,
They denied that the Moon was Stilton; they denied she
  was even Dutch.
They denied that Wishes were Horses; they denied that a
  Pig had Wings.
So we worshipped the Gods of the Market Who promised
  these beautiful things.

When the Cambrian measures were forming, They promi-
  ised perpetual peace.
They swore, if we gave them our weapons, that the wars of
  the tribes would cease.
But when we disarmed They sold us and delivered us
  bound to our foe,
And the Gods of the Copybook Headings said: 'Stick to
the Devil you know.'

On the first Feminian Sandstones we were promised the
  Fuller Life
(Which started by loving our neighbour and ended by
  loving his wife)
Till our women had no more children and the men lost
  reason and faith,
And the Gods of the Copybook Headings said: 'The Wages
of Sin is Death.'

In the Carboniferous Epoch we were promised abundance
  for all,
By robbing selected Peter to pay for collective Paul;

But, though we had plenty of money, there was nothing
     our money could buy,
And the Gods of the Copybook Headings said: '*If you don't
     work you die.*'

Then the Gods of the Market tumbled, and their smooth-
     tongued wizards withdrew,
And the hearts of the meanest were humbled and began to
     believe it was true
That All is not Gold that Glitters, and Two and Two
     make Four –
And the Gods of the Copybook Headings limped up to
     explain it once more.

     .   .   .   .   .

As it will be in the future, it was at the birth of Man –
There are only four things certain since Social Progress
     began: –
That the Dog returns to his Vomit and the Sow returns to
     her Mire,
And the burnt Fool's bandaged finger goes wabbling back
     to the Fire;

And that after this is accomplished, and the brave new
     world begins
When all men are paid for existing and no man must pay
     for his sins,
As surely as Water will wet us, as surely as Fire will burn,
The Gods of the Copybook Headings with terror and
     slaughter return!

PHILIP LARKIN
1922-1986

Aubade

I work all day, and get half drunk at night.
Waking at four to soundless dark, I stare.
In time the curtain-edges will grow light.
Till then I see what's really always there:
Unresting death, a whole day nearer now,
Making all thought impossible but how
And where and when I shall myself die.
Arid interrogation: yet the dread
Of dying, and being dead,
Flashes afresh to hold and horrify.

The mind blanks at the glare. Not in remorse
 – The good not done, the love not given, time
Torn off unused – nor wretchedly because
An only life can take so long to climb
Clear of its wrong beginnings, and may never;
But at the total emptiness for ever,
The sure extinction that we travel to
And shall be lost in always. Not to be here,
Not to be anywhere,
And soon; nothing more terrible, nothing more true.

This is a special way of being afraid
No trick dispels. Religion used to try,
That vast moth-eaten musical brocade
Created to pretend we never die,
And specious stuff that says *No rational being*
Can fear a thing it will not feel, not seeing
That this is what we fear – no sight, no sound,
No touch or taste or smell, nothing to think with,
Nothing to love or link with,
The anaesthetic from which none come round.

And so it stays just on the edge of vision,
A small unfocused blur, a standing chill
That slows each impulse down to indecision.
Most things may never happen: this one will,
And realisation of it rages out
In furnace-fear when we are caught without
People or drink. Courage is no good:
It means not scaring others. Being brave
Lets no one off the grave.
Death is no different whined at than withstood.

Slowly light strengthens, and the room takes shape.
It stands plain as a wardrobe, what we know,
Have always known, know that we can't escape,
Yet can't accept. One side will have to go.
Meanwhile telephones crouch, getting ready to ring
In locked-up offices, and all the uncaring
Intricate rented world begins to rouse.
The sky is white as clay, with no sun.
Work has to be done.
Postmen like doctors go from house to house.

RICHARD LOVELACE
1618-1657

Cupid Far Gone

What so beyond all madness is the elf,
  Now he hath got out of himself!
  His fatal enemy the bee,
  Nor his deceiv'd artillery,
  His shackles, nor the rose's bough
Ne'er half so nettled him as he is now.

See! at's own mother he is offering,
  His finger now fits any ring:
  Old Cybele he would enjoy,
  And now the girl, and now the boy.
  He proffers Jove a back caress,
And all his love in the Antipodes.

Jealous of his chaste Psyche, raging he
  Quarrels the student Mercury;
  And with a proud submissive breath
  Offers to change his darts with Death.
  He strikes at the bright eye of day,
And Juno tumbles in her Milky Way.

The dear sweet secrets of the gods he tells,
    And with loath'd hate lov'd heaven he swells;
    Now like a fury he belies
    Myriads of pure virginities;
    And swears, with this false frenzy hurl'd,
There's not a virtuous she in all the world.

Olympus he renounces, then descends,
    And makes a friendship with the fiends;
    Bids Charon be no more a slave,
    He Argos rigg'd with stars shall have;
    And triple Cerberus from below
Must leash'd t' himself with him a-hunting go.

ROBERT LOWELL
1917-1977

Skunk Hour
For Elizabeth Bishop

Nautilus Island's hermit
heiress still lives through winter in her Spartan
cottage;
her sheep still graze above the sea.
Her son's a bishop. Her farmer
is first selectman in our village,
she's in her dotage.

Thirsting for
the hierarchic privacy
of Queen Victoria's century,
she buys up all
the eyesores facing her shore,
and lets them fall.

The season's ill —
we've lost our summer millionaire,
who seemed to leap from an L. L. Bean
catalogue. His nine-knot yawl
was auctioned off to lobstermen.
A red fox stain covers Blue Hill.

And now our fairy
decorator brightens his shop for fall,
his fishnet's filled with orange cork,

orange, his cobbler's bench and awl,
there is no money in his work,
he'd rather marry.

One dark night,
my Tudor Ford climbed the hill's skull,
I watched for love-cars. Lights turned down,
they lay together, hull to hull,
where the graveyard shelves on the town. . . .
My mind's not right.

A car radio bleats,
'Love, O careless Love . . .' I hear
my ill-spirit sob in each blood cell,
as if my hand were at its throat. . . .
I myself am hell,
nobody's here –

only skunks, that search
in the moonlight for a bite to eat.
They march on their soles up Main Street:
white stripes, moonstruck eyes' red fire
under the chalk-dry and spar spire
of the Trinitarian Church.

I stand on top
of our back steps and breathe the rich air –
a mother skunk with her column of kittens swills the garbage
pail.
She jabs her wedge-head in a cup
of sour cream, drops her ostrich tail,
and will not scare.

LOUIS MACNEICE
1907-1963

Snow

The room was suddenly rich and the great bay-
    window was
Spawning snow and pink roses against it
Soundlessly collateral and incompatible:
World is suddener than we fancy it.

World is crazier and more of it than we think,
Incorrigibly plural. I peel and portion
A tangerine and spit the pips and feel
The drunkenness of things being various.

And the fire flames with a bubbling sound for world
Is more spiteful and gay than one supposes –
On the tongue on the eyes on the ears in the palms of
    one's hands –
There is more than glass between the snow and the huge
    roses.

ANDREW MARVELL
1621-1678

To His Coy Mistress

Had we but World enough, and Time,
This coyness Lady were no crime.
We would sit down, and think which way
To walk, and pass our long Love's day.
Thou by the *Indian Ganges* side
Should'st Rubies find: I by the Tide
Of *Humber* would complain. I would
Love you ten years before the Flood:
And you should if you please refuse
Till the Conversion of the *Jews*.
My vegetable Love should grow
Vaster than Empires, and more slow.
An hundred years should go to praise
Thine Eyes, and on thy Forehead Gaze.
Two hundred to adore each Breast:
But thirty thousand to the rest.
An Age at least to every part,
And the last Age should show your Heart.
For Lady you deserve this State;
Nor would I love at lower rate.
　　But at my back I always hear
Times winged Chariot hurrying near:
And yonder all before us lie
Deserts of vast Eternity.

Thy Beauty shall no more be found,
Nor, in thy marble Vault, shall sound
My echoing song: then Worms shall try
That long preserv'd Virginity:
And your quaint Honour turn to dust;
And into ashes all my Lust.
The Grave's a fine and private place,
But none I think do there embrace.

   Now therefore, while the youthful hue
Sits on thy skin like morning dew,
And while thy willing Soul transpires
At every pore with instant Fires,
Now let us sport us while we may;
And now, like am'rous birds of prey,
Rather at once our Time devour,
Than languish in his slow-chapt pow'r.
Let us roll all our Strength, and all
Our sweetness up into one Ball:
And tear our Pleasures with rough strife,
Thorough the Iron gates of Life.
Thus, though we cannot make our Sun
Stand still, yet we will make him run.

Dirge in Woods

A wind sways the pines,
    And below
Not a breath of wild air:
Still as the mosses that glow
On the flooring and over the lines
Of the roots here and there.

The pine-tree drops its dead:
They are quiet as under the sea.
Overhead, overhead,
Rushes life in a race,
As the clouds the clouds chase:
    And we go,
And we drop like the fruits of the tree,
      Even we,
      Even so.

EDNA ST. VINCENT MILLAY
1892-1950

I, being born a woman and distressed

I, being born a woman and distressed
By all the needs and notions of my kind,
Am urged by your propinquity to find
Your person fair, and feel a certain zest
To bear your body's weight upon my breast:
So subtly is the fume of life designed,
To clarify the pulse and cloud the mind,
And leave me once again undone, possessed.
Think not for this, however, the poor treason
Of my stout blood against my staggering brain,
I shall remember you with love, or season
My scorn with pity, – let me make it plain:
I find this frenzy insufficient reason
For conversation when we meet again.

The Earthly Paradise

Of Heaven or Hell I have no power to sing,
I cannot ease the burden of your fears,
Or make quick-coming death a little thing,
Or bring again the pleasure of past years,
Nor for my words shall ye forget your tears,
Or hope again for aught that I can say,
The idle singer of an empty day.

But rather, when aweary of your mirth,
From full hearts still unsatisfied ye sigh,
And, feeling kindly unto all the earth,
Grudge every minute as it passes by,
Made the more mindful that the sweet days die –
Remember me a little then I pray,
The idle singer of an empty day.

The heavy trouble, the bewildering care
That weighs us down who live and earn our bread,
These idle verses have no power to bear;
So let me sing of names remembered,
Because they, living not, can ne'er be dead,
Or long time take their memory quite away
From us poor singers of an empty day.

Dreamer of dreams, born out of my due time,
Why should I strive to set the crooked straight?
Let it suffice me that my murmuring rhyme
Beats with light wing against the ivory gate,
Telling a tale not too importunate
To those who in the sleepy region stay,
Lulled by the singer of an empty day.

Folk say, a wizard to a northern king
At Christmas-tide such wondrous things did show,
That through one window men beheld the spring,
And through another saw the summer glow,
And through a third the fruited vines a-row,
While still, unheard, but in its wonted way,
Piped the drear wind of that December day.

So with this Earthly Paradise it is,
If ye will read aright, and pardon me,
Who strive to build a shadowy isle of bliss
Midmost the beating of the steely sea,
Where tossed about all hearts of men must be;
Whose ravening monsters mighty men shall slay,
Not the poor singer of an empty day.

EDWIN MUIR
1887-1959

One foot in Eden

One foot in Eden still, I stand
And look across the other land.
The world's great day is growing late,
Yet strange these fields that we have planted
So long with crops of love and hate.
Time's handiworks by time are haunted,
And nothing now can separate
The corn and tares compactly grown.
The armorial weed in stillness bound
About the stalk; these are our own.
Evil and good stand thick around
In the fields of charity and sin
Where we shall lead our harvest in.

Yet still from Eden springs the root
As clean as on the starting day.
Time takes the foliage and the fruit
And burns the archetypal leaf
To shapes of terror and of grief
Scattered along the winter way.
But famished field and blackened tree
Bear flowers in Eden never known.
Blossoms of grief and charity
Bloom in these darkened fields alone.

What had Eden ever to say
Of hope and faith and pity and love
Until was buried all its day
And memory found its treasure trove?
Strange blessings never in Paradise
Fall from these beclouded skies.

THOMAS NASHE
1567-1601

Adieu, farewell earth's bliss

Adieu, farewell earth's bliss,
This world uncertain is;
Fond are life's lustful joys,
Death proves them all but toys,
None from his darts can fly.
I am sick, I must die.
   Lord, have mercy on us!

Rich men, trust not in wealth,
Gold cannot buy you health;
Physic himself must fade,
All things to end are made.
The plague full swift goes by.
I am sick, I must die.
   Lord, have mercy on us!

Beauty is but a flower
Which wrinkles will devour;
Brightness falls from the air,
Queens have died young and fair,
Dust hath clos'd Helen's eye.
I am sick, I must die.
   Lord, have mercy on us!

Strength stoops unto the grave,
Worms feed on Hector brave,
Swords may not fight with fate,
Earth still holds ope her gate.
Come! come! the bells do cry.
I am sick, I must die.
    Lord, have mercy on us!

Wit with his wantonness
Tasteth death's bitterness;
Hell's executioner
Hath no ears for to hear
What vain art can reply.
I am sick, I must die.
    Lord, have mercy on us!

Haste, therefore, each degree,
To welcome destiny.
Heaven is our heritage,
Earth but a player's stage;
Mount we unto the sky.
I am sick, I must die.
    Lord, have mercy on us!

The Parable of the Old Man and the Young

So Abram rose, and clave the wood, and went,
And took the fire with him, and a knife.
And as they sojourned both of them together,
Isaac the first-born spake and said, My Father,
Behold the preparations, fire and iron,
But where the lamb for this burnt-offering?
Then Abram bound the youth with belts and straps,
And builded parapets and trenches there,
And stretchèd forth the knife to slay his son.
When lo! an angel called him out of heaven,
Saying, Lay not thy hand upon the lad,
Neither do anything to him. Behold,
A ram, caught in a thicket by its horns;
Offer the Ram of Pride instead of him.
But the old man would not so, but slew his son, –
And half the seed of Europe, one by one.

Daddy

You do not do, you do not do
Any more, black shoe
In which I have lived like a foot
For thirty years, poor and white,
Barely daring to breathe or Achoo.

Daddy, I have had to kill you.
You died before I had time –
Marble-heavy, a bag full of God,
Ghastly statue with one grey toe
Big as a Frisco seal

And a head in the freakish Atlantic
Where it pours bean green over blue
In the waters off beautiful Nauset.
I used to pray to recover you.
Ach, du.

In the German tongue, in the Polish town
Scraped flat by the roller
Of wars, wars, wars.
But the name of the town is common.
My Polack friend

Says there are a dozen or two.
So I never could tell where you
Put your foot, your root,
I never could talk to you.
The tongue stuck in my jaw.

It stuck in a barb wire snare.
Ich, ich, ich, ich,
I could hardly speak.
I thought every German was you.
And the language obscene

An engine, an engine
Chuffing me off like a Jew.
A Jew to Dachau, Auschwitz, Belsen.
I began to talk like a Jew.
I think I may well be a Jew.

The snows of the Tyrol, the clear beer of Vienna
Are not very pure or true.
With my gypsy ancestress and my weird luck
And my Taroc pack and my Taroc pack
I may be a bit of a Jew.

I have always been scared of *you*,
With your Luftwaffe, your gobbledygoo.
And your neat moustache
And your Aryan eye, bright blue.
Panzer-man, panzer-man, O You –

Not God but a swastika
So black no sky could squeak through.
Every woman adores a Fascist,
The boot in the face, the brute
Brute heart of a brute like you.

You stand at the blackboard, daddy,
In the picture I have of you,
A cleft in your chin instead of your foot
But no less a devil for that, no not
Any less the black man who

Bit my pretty red heart in two.
I was ten when they buried you.
At twenty I tried to die
And get back, back, back to you.
I thought even the bones would do.

But they pulled me out of the sack,
And they stuck me together with glue.
And then I knew what to do.
I made a model of you,
A man in black with a Meinkampf look.

And a love of the rack and the screw.
And I said I do, I do.
So daddy, I'm finally through.
The black telephone's off at the root,
The voices just can't worm through.

If I've killed one man, I've killed two –
The vampire who said he was you
And drank my blood for a year,
Seven years, if you want to know.
Daddy, you can lie back now.

There's a stake in your fat black heart
And the villagers never liked you.
They are dancing and stamping on you.
They always *knew* it was you.
Daddy, daddy, you bastard, I'm through.

Annabel Lee

It was many and many a year ago,
    In a kingdom by the sea,
That a maiden there lived whom you may know
    By the name of Annabel Lee;
And this maiden she lived with no other thought
    Than to love and be loved by me.

She was a child and *I* was a child,
    In this kingdom by the sea,
But we loved with a love that was more than love –
    I and my Annabel Lee –
With a love that the wingèd seraphs of Heaven
    Coveted her and me.

And this was the reason that, long ago,
    In this kingdom by the sea,
A wind blew out of a cloud by night
    Chilling my Annabel Lee;
So that her highborn kinsmen came
    And bore her away from me,
To shut her up in a sepulchre
    In this kingdom by the sea.

The angels, not half so happy in Heaven,
     Went envying her and me: –
Yes! – that was the reason (as all men know,
     In this kingdom by the sea)
That the wind came out of the cloud, chilling
     And killing my Annabel Lee.

But our love it was stronger by far than the love
     Of those who were older than we –
     Of many far wiser than we –
And neither the angels in Heaven above
   Nor the demons down under the sea,
Can ever dissever my soul from the soul
     Of the beautiful Annabel Lee: –

For the moon never beams, without bringing me dreams
     Of the beautiful Annabel Lee;
And the stars never rise but I see the bright eyes
     Of the beautiful Annabel Lee:
And so, all the night-tide, I lie down by the side
Of my darling, my darling, my life and my bride,
     In her sepulchre there by the sea –
     In her tomb by the side of the sea.

ALEXANDER POPE
1688-1744

Epistle to Miss Blount, on Her Leaving the Town, after the Coronation

As some fond virgin, whom her mother's care
Drags from the town to wholsome country air,
Just when she learns to roll a melting eye,
And hear a spark, yet think no danger nigh;
From the dear man unwilling she must sever,
Yet takes one kiss before she parts for ever:
Thus from the world fair *Zephalinda* flew,
Saw·others happy, and with sighs withdrew;
Not that their pleasures caus'd her discontent,
She sigh'd not that They stay'd, but that She went.

   She went, to plain-work, and to purling brooks,
Old-fashion'd halls, dull aunts, and croaking rooks,
She went from Op'ra, park, assembly, play,
To morning walks, and pray'rs three hours a day;
To pass her time 'twixt reading and Bohea,
To muse, and spill her solitary Tea,
Or o'er cold coffee trifle with the spoon,
Count the slow clock, and dine exact at noon;
Divert her eyes with pictures in the fire,
Hum half a tune, tell stories to the squire;
Up to her godly garret after sev'n,
There starve and pray, for that's the way to heav'n.

Some Squire, perhaps, you take a delight to rack;
Whose game is Whisk, whose treat a toast in sack,
Who visits with a gun, presents you birds,
Then gives a smacking buss, and cries – No words!
Or with his hound comes hollowing from the stable,
Makes love with nods, and knees beneath a table;
Whose laughs are hearty, tho' his jests are coarse,
And loves you best of all things – but his horse.
   In some fair evening, on your elbow laid,
You dream of triumphs in the rural shade;
In pensive thought recall the fancy'd scene,
See Coronations rise on ev'ry green;
Before you pass th' imaginary sights
Of Lords, and Earls, and Dukes, and garter'd Knights,
While the spread Fan o'ershades your closing eyes;
Then give one flirt, and all the vision flies.
Thus vanish sceptres, coronets, and balls,
And leave you in lone woods, or empty walls.
   So when your slave, at some dear, idle time,
(Not plagu'd with headaches, or the want of rhyme)
Stands in the streets, abstracted from the crew,
And while he seems to study, thinks of you:
Just when his fancy points your sprightly eyes,
Or sees the blush of soft *Parthenia* rise,
Gay pats my shoulder, and you vanish quite;
Streets, chairs, and coxcombs rush upon my sight;
Vex'd to be still in town, I knit my brow,
Look sour, and hum a tune – as you may now.

Commission

Go, my songs, to the lonely and the unsatisfied,
Go also to the nerve-racked, go to the enslaved-by-
                                        convention,
Bear to them my contempt for their oppressors.
Go as a great wave of cool water,
Bear my contempt of oppressors.

Speak against unconscious oppression,
Speak against the tyranny of the unimaginative,
Speak against bonds.
Go to the bourgeoise who is dying of her ennuis,
Go to the women in suburbs.
Go to the hideously wedded,
Go to them whose failure is concealed,
Go to the unluckily mated,
Go to the bought wife,
Go to the woman entailed.

Go to those who have delicate lust,
Go to those whose delicate desires are thwarted,
Go like a blight upon the dullness of the world;
Go with your edge against this,
Strengthen the subtle cords,
Bring confidence upon the algæ and the tentacles of the
                                        soul.

Go in a friendly manner,
Go with an open speech.
Be eager to find new evils and new good,
Be against all forms of oppression.
Go to those who are thickened with middle age,
To those who have lost their interest.

Go to the adolescent who are smothered in family –
Oh how hideous it is
To see three generations of one house gathered together!
It is like an old tree with shoots,
And with some branches rotted and falling.

Go out and defy opinion,
Go against this vegetable bondage of the blood.
Be against all sorts of mortmain.

SIR WALTER RALEGH
1552-1618

The Lie

Go, soul, the body's guest,
Upon a thankless arrant,
Fear not to touch the best,
The truth shall be thy warrant:
Go, since I needs must die,
And give the world the lie.

Say to the court it glows
And shines like rotten wood;
Say to the church, it shows
What's good, and doth no good:
If church and court reply,
Then give them both the lie.

Tell potentates, they live
Acting by others' action,
Not lov'd unless they give,
Not strong but by affection:
If potentates reply,
Give potentates the lie.

Tell men of high condition,
That manage the estate,
Their purpose is ambition,
Their practice only hate:
And if they once reply,
Then give them all the lie.

Tell them that brave it most,
They beg for more by spending,
Who in their greatest cost
Seek nothing but commending.
And if they make reply,
Then give them all the lie.

Tell zeal it wants devotion,
Tell love it is but lust,
Tell time it is but motion,
Tell flesh it is but dust.
And wish them not reply,
For thou must give the lie.

Tell age it daily wasteth,
Tell honour how it alters,
Tell beauty how she blasteth,
Tell favour how it falters,
And as they shall reply,
Give every one the lie.

Tell wit how much it wrangles
In tickle points of niceness,
Tell wisdom she entangles
Herself in over-wiseness.
And when they do reply,
Straight give them both the lie.

Tell physic of her boldness,
Tell skill it is prevention;
Tell charity of coldness,
Tell law it is contention,
And as they do reply,
So give them still the lie.

Tell fortune of her blindness,
Tell nature of decay,
Tell friendship of unkindness,
Tell justice of delay;
And if they will reply,
Then give them all the lie.

Tell arts they have no soundness,
But vary by esteeming,
Tell schools they want profoundness
And stand too much on seeming.
If arts and schools reply,
Give arts and schools the lie.

Tell faith it's fled the city,
Tell how the country erreth,
Tell manhood shakes off pity,
And virtue least preferreth,
And if they do reply,
Spare not to give the lie.

So when thou hast, as I
Commanded thee, done blabbing,
 – Although to give the lie,
Deserves no less than stabbing –
Stab at thee he that will,
No stab the soul can kill.

JOHN CROWE RANSOM
1888-1974

Piazza Piece

‒ I am a gentleman in a dustcoat trying
To make you hear. Your ears are soft and small
And listen to an old man not at all,
They want the young men's whispering and sighing.
But see the roses on your trellis dying
And hear the spectral singing of the moon;
For I must have my lovely lady soon,
I am a gentleman in a dustcoat trying.

‒ I am a lady young in beauty waiting
Until my truelove comes, and then we kiss.
But what grey man among the vines is this
Whose words are dry and faint as in a dream?
Back from my trellis, Sir, before I scream!
I am a lady young in beauty waiting.

JOHN WILMOT, EARL OF ROCHESTER
1647-1680

A Song of a Young Lady to Her Ancient Lover

Ancient Person, for whom I
All the flatt'ring Youth defy;
Long be it e're thou grow old,
Aching, shaking, crazy, cold.
But still continue as thou art,
Ancient Person of my Heart.

On thy wither'd lips and dry,
Which like barren furrows lie,
Brooding kisses I will pour,
Shall thy youthful heart restore.
(Such kind showers in autumn fall,
And a second spring recall);
Nor from thee will ever part,
Ancient Person of my Heart.

Thy nobler part, which but to name,
In our sex would be counted shame,
By age's frozen grasp possess'd,
From his ice shall be releas'd,
And, sooth'd by my reviving hand,
In former warmth and vigour stand.
All a lover's wish can reach,
For thy joy my love shall teach,
And for thy pleasure shall improve
All that Art can add to Love.
Yet still I love thee without Art,
Ancient Person of my Heart.

THEODORE ROETHKE
1908-1963

The Waking

I wake to sleep, and take my waking slow.
I feel my fate in what I cannot fear.
I learn by going where I have to go.

We think by feeling. What is there to know?
I hear my being dance from ear to ear.
I wake to sleep, and take my waking slow.

Of those so close beside me, which are you?
God bless the Ground! I shall walk softly there,
And learn by going where I have to go.

Light takes the Tree; but who can tell us how?
The lowly worm climbs up a winding stair;
I wake to sleep, and take my waking slow.

Great Nature has another thing to do
To you and me; so take the lively air,
And, lovely, learn by going where to go.

This shaking keeps me steady. I should know.
What falls away is always. And is near.
I wake to sleep, and take my waking slow.
I learn by going where I have to go.

August 1914

What in our lives is burnt
In the fire of this?
The heart's dear granary?
The much we shall miss?

Three lives hath one life –
Iron, honey, gold.
The gold, the honey gone –
Left is the hard and cold.

Iron are our lives
Molten right through our youth.
A burnt space through ripe fields
A fair mouth's broken tooth.

CHRISTINA ROSSETTI
1830-1894

What Would I Give?

What would I give for a heart of flesh to warm me through,
Instead of this heart of stone ice-cold whatever I do;
Hard and cold and small, of all hearts the worst of all.

What would I give for words, if only words would come;
But now in its misery my spirit has fallen dumb:
Oh, merry friends, go your way, I have never a word to
                                                    say.

What would I give for tears, not smiles but scalding tears,
To wash the black mark clean, and to thaw the frost of
                                                    years,
To wash the stain ingrain and to make me clean again.

DANTE GABRIEL ROSSETTI
1828-1882

Sudden Light

I have been here before,
　　But when or how I cannot tell:
I know the grass beyond the door,
　　The sweet keen smell,
The sighing sound, the lights around the shore.

You have been mine before, –
　　How long ago I may not know:
But just when at that swallow's soar
　　Your neck turned so,
Some veil did fall, – I knew it all of yore.

Has this been thus before?
　　And shall not thus time's eddying flight
Still with our lives our love restore
　　In death's despite,
And day and night yield one delight once more?

DELMORE SCHWARTZ
1913-1966

Calmly we walk through this April's day

Calmly we walk through this April's day,
Metropolitan poetry here and there,
In the park sit pauper and *rentier*,
The screaming children, the motor-car
Fugitive about us, running away,
Between the worker and the millionaire
Number provides all distances,
It is Nineteen Thirty-Seven now,
Many great dears are taken away,
What will become of you and me
(This is the school in which we learn . . .)
Besides the photo and the memory?
(. . . that time is the fire in which we burn.)

(This is the school in which we learn . . .)
What is the self amid this blaze?
What am I now that I was then
Which I shall suffer and act again,
The theodicy I wrote in my high school days
Restored all life from infancy,
The children shouting are bright as they run
(This is the school in which they learn . . .)
Ravished entirely in their passing play!
(. . . that time is the fire in which they burn.)

Avid its rush, that reeling blaze!
Where is my father and Eleanor?
Not where are they now, dead seven years,
But what they were then?
                    No more? No more?
From Nineteen-Fourteen to the present day,
Bert Spira and Rhoda consume, consume
Not where they are now (where are they now?)
But what they were then, both beautiful;
Each minute bursts in the burning room,
The great globe reels in the solar fire,
Spinning the trivial and unique away.
(How all things flash! How all things flare!)
What am I now that I was then?
May memory restore again and again
The smallest color of the smallest day:
Time is the school in which we learn,
Time is the fire in which we burn.

SIR CHARLES SEDLEY
1639-1701

On a Cock at Rochester

Thou cursed Cock, with thy perpetual Noise,
May'st thou be Capon made, and lose thy Voice,
Or on a dunghill may'st thou spend thy Blood,
And Vermin prey upon thy craven Brood;
May Rivals tread thy Hens before thy Face,
Then with redoubled Courage give thee chase;
May'st thou be punish'd for St. *Peter's* Crime,
And on *Shrove-tuesday*, perish in thy Prime;
May thy bruis'd Carcass be some Beggar's Feast,
Thou first and worst Disturber of Man's Rest.

ANNE SEXTON
1928-1974

All My Pretty Ones

All my pretty ones?
Did you say all? O hell-kite! All?
What! all my pretty chickens and their dam
At one fell swoop? . . .
I cannot but remember such things were,
That were most precious to me.

– Macbeth

Father, this year's jinx rides us apart
where you followed our mother to her cold slumber,
a second shock boiling its stone to your heart,
leaving me here to shuffle and disencumber
you from the residence you could not afford:
a gold key, your half of a woollen mill,
twenty suits from Dunne's, an English Ford,
the love and legal verbiage of another will,
boxes of pictures of people I do not know.
I touch their cardboard faces. They must go.

But the eyes, as thick as wood in this album,
hold me. I stop here, where a small boy
waits in a ruffled dress for someone to come . . .
for this soldier who holds his bugle like a toy
or for this velvet lady who cannot smile.
Is this your father's father, this commodore
in a mailman suit? My father, time meanwhile
has made it unimportant who you are looking for.
I'll never know what these faces are all about.
I lock them into their book and throw them out.

This is the yellow scrapbook that you began
the year I was born; as crackling now and wrinkly
as tobacco leaves: clippings where Hoover outran
the Democrats, wriggling his dry finger at me
and Prohibition; news where the *Hindenburg* went
down and recent years where you went flush
on war. This year, solvent but sick, you meant
to marry that pretty widow in a one-month rush.
But before you had that second chance, I cried
on your fat shoulder. Three days later you died.

These are the snapshots of marriage, stopped in places.
Side by side at the rail toward Nassau now;
here, with the winner's cup at the speedboat races,
here, in tails at the Cotillion, you take a bow,
here, by our kennel of dogs with their pink eyes,
running like show-bred pigs in their chain-link pen;
here, at the horseshow where my sister wins a prize;
and here, standing like a duke among groups of men.
Now I fold you down, my drunkard, my navigator,
my first lost keeper, to love or look at later.

I hold a five-year diary that my mother kept
for three years, telling all she does not say
of your alcoholic tendency. You overslept,
she writes. My God, father, each Christmas Day
with your blood, will I drink down your glass
of wine? The diary of your hurly-burly years
goes to my shelf to wait for my age to pass.
Only in this hoarded span will love persevere.
Whether you are pretty or not, I outlive you,
bend down my strange face to yours and forgive you.

WILLIAM SHAKESPEARE
1564-1616

When, in disgrace with fortune and men's eyes

When, in disgrace with fortune and men's eyes,
    I all alone beweep my outcast state,
And trouble deaf heaven with my bootless cries,
    And look upon myself, and curse my fate,
Wishing me like to one more rich in hope,
    Featured like him, like him with friends possessed,
Desiring this man's art and that man's scope,
    With what I most enjoy contented least;
Yet in these thoughts myself almost despising,
    Haply I think on thee, and then my state,
Like to the lark at break of day arising
    From sullen earth, sings hymns at heaven's gate;
        For thy sweet love remembered such wealth brings
        That then I scorn to change my state with kings.

PERCY BYSSHE SHELLEY
1792-1822

To . . . .

One word is too often profaned
　　For me to profane it,
One feeling too falsely disdained
　　For thee to disdain it;
One hope is too like despair
　　For prudence to smother,
And pity from thee more dear
　　Than that from another.

I can give not what men call love,
　　But wilt thou accept not
The worship the heart lifts above
　　And the Heavens reject not, –
The desire of the moth for the star,
　　Of the night for the morrow,
The devotion to something afar
　　From the sphere of our sorrow?

SIR PHILIP SIDNEY
1554-1586

Loving in truth, and fain in verse my love to show

Loving in truth, and fain in verse my love to show,
That She, dear She, might take some pleasure of my pain,
Pleasure might cause her read, reading might make her
know,
Knowledge might pity win, and pity grace obtain,
I sought fit words to paint the blackest face of woe;
Studying inventions fine, her wits to entertain,
Oft turning others' leaves, to see if thence would flow
Some fresh and fruitful showers upon my sun-burn'd brain.
But words came halting out, wanting Invention's stay;
Invention, Nature's child, fled stepdame Study's blows;
And others' feet still seem'd but strangers in my way.
Thus, great with child to speak, and helpless in my throes,
Biting my truand pen, beating myself for spite,
'Fool,' said my Muse to me, 'look in thy heart and write.'

Sir Beelzebub

When
Sir
Beelzebub called for his syllabub in the hotel in Hell
      Where Proserpine first fell,
Blue as the gendarmerie were the waves of the sea,
      (Rocking and shocking the barmaid).

Nobody comes to give him his rum but the
Rim of the sky hippopotamus-glum
Enhances the chances to bless with a benison
Alfred Lord Tennyson crossing the bar laid
With cold vegetation from pale deputations
Of temperance workers (all signed In Memoriam)
Hoping with glory to trip up the Laureate's feet,
      (Moving in classical metres) . . .

Like Balaclava, the lava came down from the
Roof, and the sea's blue wooden gendarmerie
Took them in charge while Beelzebub roared for his rum.
      . . . None of them come!

JOHN SKELTON
1460-1529

To Mistress Margaret Hussey

Merry Margaret,
   As midsummer flower,
Gentle as falcon
Or hawk of the tower:
With solace and gladness,
Much mirth and no madness,
All good and no badness;
   So joyously,
   So maidenly,
   So womanly
   Her demeaning
   In every thing,
   Far, far passing
   That I can indite,
   Or suffice to write
Of Merry Margaret
   As midsummer flower,
Gentle as falcon
Or hawk of the tower.

As patient and still
And as full of good will
As fair Isaphill,
Coriander,
Sweet pomander,
Good Cassander,
Steadfast of thought,
Well made, well wrought,
   Far may be sought
   Ere that ye can find
   So courteous, so kind
   As Merry Margaret,
      This midsummer flower,
   Gentle as falcon
   Or hawk of the tower.

STEVIE SMITH
1902–1971

To the Tune of the Coventry Carol

The nearly right
And yet not quite
In love is wholly evil
And every heart
That loves in part
Is mortgaged to the devil.

I loved or thought
I loved in sort
Was this to love akin
To take the best
And leave the rest
And let the devil in?

O lovers true
And others too
Whose best is only better
Take my advice
Shun compromise
Forget him and forget her.

EDMUND SPENSER
1552-1599

Iambicum Trimetrum

Unhappy verse, the witness of my unhappy state,
  make thyself fluttering wings of thy fast flying
  thought, and fly forth unto my love, whereso'er she be:

Whether lying restless in heavy bed, or else
  sitting so cheerless at the cheerful board, or else
  playing alone careless on her heavenly virginals.

If in bed, tell her that my eyes can take no rest;
  if at board, tell her that my mouth can eat no meat;
  if at her virginals, tell her I can hear no mirth.

Asked why, say waking love suffereth no sleep;
  say that raging love doth appal the weak stomach;
  say that lamenting love marreth the musical.

Tell her that her pleasures were wont to lull me asleep;
  tell her that her beauty was wont to feed mine eyes;
  tell her that her sweet tongue was wont to make me
                              mirth.

Now do I nightly waste, wanting my kindly rest;
  now do I daily starve, wanting my lively food;
  now do I always die, wanting my timely mirth.

And if I waste, who will bewail my heavy chance?
and if I starve, who will record my cursed end?
and if I die, who will say: *This was Immerito?*

WALLACE STEVENS
1879-1955

The Emperor of Ice-Cream

Call the roller of big cigars,
The muscular one, and bid him whip
In kitchen cups concupiscent curds.
Let the wenches dawdle in such dress
As they are used to wear, and let the boys
Bring flowers in last month's newspapers.
Let be be finale of seem.
The only emperor is the emperor of ice-cream.

Take from the dresser of deal,
Lacking the three glass knobs, that sheet
On which she embroidered fantails once
And spread it so as to cover her face.
If her horny feet protrude, they come
To show how cold she is, and dumb.
Let the lamp affix its beam.
The only emperor is the emperor of ice-cream.

SIR JOHN SUCKLING
1609-1642

Song

Why so pale and wan, fond lover?
    Prithee, why so pale?
Will, when looking well can't move her,
    Looking ill prevail?
    Prithee, why so pale?

Why so dull and mute, young sinner?
    Prithee, why so mute?
Will, when speaking well can't win her,
    Saying nothing do't?
    Prithee, why so mute?

Quit, quit, for shame; this will not move,
    This cannot take her;
If of herself she will not love,
    Nothing can make her:
    The devil take her!

A Beautiful Young Nymph Going to Bed

Corinna, Pride of *Drury-Lane*,
For whom no Shepherd sighs in vain;
Never did Covent Garden boast
So bright a batter'd, strolling Toast;
No drunken Rake to pick her up,
No Cellar where on Tick to sup;
Returning at the Midnight Hour;
Four Stories climbing to her Bow'r;
Then, seated on a three-legg'd Chair,
Takes off her artificial Hair:
Now, picking out a Crystal Eye,
She wipes it clean, and lays it by.
Her Eye-Brows from a Mouse's Hide,
Stuck on with Art on either Side,
Pulls off with Care, and first displays 'em,
Then in a Play-Book smoothly lays 'em.
Now dextrously her Plumpers draws,
That serve to fill her hollow Jaws.
Untwists a Wire; and from her Gums
A Set of Teeth completely comes.
Pulls out the Rags contriv'd to prop
Her flabby Dugs and down they drop.

Proceeding on, the lovely Goddess
Unlaces next her Steel-Rib'd Bodice;
Which by the Operator's Skill,
Press down the Lumps, the Hollows fill,
Up goes her Hand, and off she slips
The Bolsters that supply her Hips.
With gentlest Touch, she next explores
Her Shankers, Issues, running Sores,
Effects of many a sad Disaster;
And then to each applies a Plaster.
But must, before she goes to Bed,
Rub off the Daubs of White and Red;
And smooth the Furrows in her Front,
With greasy Paper stuck upon't.
She takes a *Bolus* e'er she sleeps;
And then between two Blankets creeps.
With Pains of Love tormented lies;
Or if she chance to close her Eyes,
Of *Bridewell* and the *Compter* dreams,
And feels the Lash, and faintly screams;
Or, by a faithless Bully drawn,
At some Hedge-Tavern lies in Pawn;
Or to *Jamaica* seems transported,
Alone, and by no Planter courted;
Or, near *Fleet-Ditch's* oozy Brinks,
Surrounded with a Hundred Stinks,
Belated, seems on watch to lie,
And snap some Cully passing by;
Or, struck with Fear, her Fancy runs
On Watchmen, Constables and Duns,
From whom she meets with frequent Rubs;
But, never from Religious Clubs;

Whose Favour she is sure to find,
Because she pays them all in Kind.
   CORINNA wakes. A dreadful Sight!
Behold the Ruins of the Night!
A wicked Rat her Plaster stole,
Half eat, and dragg'd it to his Hole.
The Crystal Eye, alas, was miss'd;
And *Puss* had on her Plumpers piss'd.
A Pigeon pick'd her Issue-Peas;
And *Shock* her Tresses fill'd with Fleas.
   The Nymph, tho' in this mangled Plight,
Must ev'ry Morn her Limbs unite.
But how shall I describe her Arts
To recollect the scatter'd Parts?
Or show the Anguish, Toil, and Pain,
Of gath'ring up herself again?
The bashful Muse will never bear
In such a Scene to interfere.
Corinna in the Morning dizen'd,
Who sees, will spew; who smells, be poison'd.

ALGERNON CHARLES SWINBURNE
1837–1909

A Leave-Taking

Let us go hence, my songs; she will not hear.
Let us go hence together without fear;
Keep silence now, for singing-time is over,
And over all old things and all things dear.
She loves not you nor me as all we love her.
Yea, though we sang as angels in her ear,
     She would not hear.

Let us rise up and part; she will not know.
Let us go seaward as the great winds go,
Full of blown sand and foam; what help is here?
There is no help, for all these things are so,
And all the world is bitter as a tear.
And how these things are, though ye strove to show,
     She would not know.

Let us go home and hence; she will not weep.
We gave love many dreams and days to keep,
Flowers without scent, and fruits that would not grow,
Saying 'If thou wilt, thrust in thy sickle and reap.'
All is reaped now; no grass is left to mow;
And we that sowed, though all we fell on sleep,
     She would not weep.

Let us go hence and rest; she will not love,
She shall not hear us if we sing hereof,
Nor see love's ways, how sore they are and steep.
Come hence, let be, lie still; it is enough.
Love is a barren sea, bitter and deep;
And though she saw all heaven in flower above,
        She would not love.

Let us give up, go down; she will not care.
Though all the stars made gold of all the air,
And the sea moving saw before it move
One moon-flower making all the foam-flowers fair;
Though all those waves went over us, and drove
Deep down the stifling lips and drowning hair,
        She would not care.

Let us go hence, go hence; she will not see.
Sing all once more together; surely she,
She too, remembering days and words that were,
Will turn a little toward us, sighing; but we,
We are hence, we are gone, as though we had not been
                                              there.
Nay, and though all men seeing had pity on me,
        She would not see.

ALFRED, LORD TENNYSON
1809-1892

Vastness

i
Many a hearth upon our dark globe sighs
    after many a vanish'd face,
Many a planet by many a sun may roll with
    the dust of a vanish'd race.

ii
Raving politics, never at rest – as this poor
    earth's pale history runs, –
What is it all but a trouble of ants in the
    gleam of a million million of suns?

iii
Lies upon this side, lies upon that side,
    truthless violence mourn'd by the Wise,
Thousands of voices drowning his own in
    a popular torrent of lies upon lies;

iv
Stately purposes, valour in battle, glorious
    annals of army and fleet,
Death for the right cause, death for the
    wrong cause, trumpets of victory, groans of defeat;

Innocence seethed in her mother's milk,
　　and Charity setting the martyr aflame;
Thraldom who walks with the banner of
　　Freedom, and recks not to ruin a realm in her name.

vi

Faith at her zenith, or all but lost in the
　　gloom of doubts that darken the schools;
Craft with a bunch of all-heal in her hand,
　　follow'd up by her vassal legion of fools;

vii

Trade flying over a thousand seas with her
　　spice and her vintage, her silk and her corn;
Desolate offing, sailorless harbours, famishing
　　populace, wharves forlorn;

viii

Star of the morning, Hope in the sunrise;
　　gloom of the evening, Life at a close;
Pleasure who flaunts on her wide down-
　　way with her flying robe and her poison'd rose;

ix

Pain, that has crawl'd from the corpse of
　　Pleasure, a worm which writhes all day, and at night
Stirs up again in the heart of the sleeper,
　　and stings him back to the curse of the light;

Wealth with his wines and his wedded harlots;
    honest Poverty, bare to the bone;
Opulent Avarice, lean as Poverty; Flattery
    gilding the rift in a throne;

xi

Fame blowing out from her golden trumpet
    a jubilant challenge to Time and to Fate;
Slander, her shadow, sowing the nettle on
    all the laurel'd graves of the Great;

xii

Love for the maiden, crown'd with marriage,
    no regrets for aught that has been,
Household happiness, gracious children,
    debtless competence, golden mean;

xiii

National hatreds of whole generations, and
    pigmy spites of the village spire;
Vows that will last to the last death-ruckle,
    and vows that are snapt in a moment of fire;

xiv

He that has lived for the lust of the minute,
    and died in the doing it, flesh without mind;
He that has nail'd all flesh to the Cross, till
    Self died out in the love of his kind;

Spring and Summer and Autumn and
    Winter, and all these old revolutions of earth;
All new-old revolutions of Empire –
    change of the tide – what is all of it worth?

What the philosophies, all the sciences,
    poesy, varying voices of prayer?
All that is noblest, all that is basest, all that
    is filthy with all that is fair?

What is it all, if we all of us end but
    being our own corpse-coffins at last,
Swallow'd in Vastness, lost in Silence,
    drown'd in the deeps of a meaningless Past?

What but a murmur of gnats in the gloom
    or a moment's anger of bees in their hive? –

★   ★   ★   ★   ★

Peace, let it be! for I loved him, and love
    him for ever: the dead are not dead but alive.

DYLAN THOMAS
1914-1953

Lament

When I was a windy boy and a bit
And the black spit of the chapel fold,
(Sighed the old ram rod, dying of women),
I tiptoed shy in the gooseberry wood,
The rude owl cried like a telltale tit,
I skipped in a blush as the big girls rolled
Ninepin down on the donkeys' common,
And on seesaw sunday nights I wooed
Whoever I would with my wicked eyes,
The whole of the moon I could love and leave
All the green leaved little weddings' wives
In the coal black bush and let them grieve.

When I was a gusty man and a half
And the black beast of the beetles' pews,
(Sighed the old ram rod, dying of bitches),
Not a boy and a bit in the wick-
Dipping moon and drunk as a new dropped calf,
I whistled all night in the twisted flues,
Midwives grew in the midnight ditches,
And the sizzling beds of the town cried, Quick! –
Whenever I dove in a breast high shoal,
Wherever I ramped in the clover quilts,
Whatsoever I did in the coal –
Black night, I left my quivering prints.

When I was a man you could call a man
And the black cross of the holy house,
(Sighed the old ram rod, dying of welcome),
Brandy and ripe in my bright, bass prime,
No springtailed tom in the red hot town
With every simmering woman his mouse
But a hillocky bull in the swelter
Of summer come in his great good time
To the sultry, biding herds, I said,
Oh, time enough when the blood creeps cold,
And I lie down but to sleep in bed,
For my sulking, skulking, coal black soul!

When I was a half of the man I was
And serve me right as the preachers warn,
(Sighed the old ram rod, dying of downfall),
No flailing calf or cat in a flame
Or hickory bull in milky grass
But a black sheep with a crumpled horn,
At last the soul from its foul mousehole
Slunk pouting out when the limp time came;
And I gave my soul a blind, slashed eye,
Gristle and rind, and a roarers' life,
And I shoved it into the coal black sky
To find a woman's soul for a wife.

Now I am a man no more no more
And a black reward for a roaring life,
(Sighed the old ram rod, dying of strangers),
Tidy and cursed in my dove cooed room
I lie down thin and hear the good bells jaw –
For, oh, my soul found a sunday wife
In the coal black sky and she bore angels!
Harpies around me out of her womb!
Chastity prays for me, piety sings,
Innocence sweetens my last black breath,
Modesty hides my thighs in her wings,
And all the deadly virtues plague my death!

CHIDIOCK TICHBORNE
d. 1586

My prime of youth is but a frost of cares

My prime of youth is but a frost of cares;
  My feast of joy is but a dish of pain;
My crop of corn is but a field of tares;
  And all my good is but vain hope of gain;
My life is fled, and yet I saw no sun;
And now I live, and now my life is done.

The spring is past, and yet it hath not sprung;
  The fruit is dead, and yet the leaves be green;
My youth is gone, and yet I am but young;
  I saw the world and yet I was not seen;
My thread is cut, and yet it is not spun;
And now I live, and now my life is done.

I sought my death and found it in my womb,
  I look'd for life and saw it was a shade,
I trod the earth and knew it was my tomb,
  And now I die, and now I was but made;
My glass is full, and now my glass is run,
And now I live, and now my life is done.

EDMUND WALLER
1606-1687

Go, lovely Rose

Go, lovely Rose –
Tell her that wastes her time and me,
    That now she knows,
When I resemble her to thee,
How sweet and fair she seems to be.

    Tell her that's young,
And shuns to have her graces spied,
    That hadst thou sprung
In deserts where no men abide,
Thou must have uncommended died.

    Small is the worth
Of beauty from the light retired:
    Bid her come forth,
Suffer herself to be desired,
And not blush so to be admired.

    Then die – that she
The common fate of all things rare
    May read in thee;
How small a part of time they share
That are so wondrous sweet and fair!

WALT WHITMAN
1819–1892

Native Moments

Native moments – when you come upon me – ah you are
                             here now,
Give me now libidinous joys only,
Give me the drench of my passions, give me life coarse and
                                 rank,
To-day I go consort with Nature's darlings, to-night too,
I am for those who believe in loose delights, I share the
                       midnight orgies of young men,
I dance with the dancers and drink with the drinkers,
The echoes ring with our indecent calls, I pick out some
                  low person for my dearest friend,
He shall be lawless, rude, illiterate, he shall be one
                condemned by others for deeds done,
I will play a part no longer, why should I exile myself from
                    my companions?
O you shunn'd persons, I at least do not shun you,
I come forthwith in your midst, I will be your poet,
I will be more to you than to any of the rest.

WILLIAM WORDSWORTH
1770–1850

Mutability

From low to high doth dissolution climb,
And sink from high to low, along a scale
Of awful notes, whose concord shall not fail;
A musical but melancholy chime,
Which they can hear who meddle not with crime,
Nor avarice, nor over-anxious care.
Truth fails not; but her outward forms that bear
The longest date do melt like frosty rime,
That in the morning whitened hill and plain
And is no more; drop like the tower sublime
Of yesterday, which royally did wear
His crown of weeds, but could not even sustain
Some casual shout that broke the silent air,
Or the unimaginable touch of Time.

JAMES WRIGHT
1927-1980

Lying in a Hammock at William Duffy's Farm in Pine Island, Minnesota

Over my head, I see the bronze butterfly,
Asleep on the black trunk,
Blowing like a leaf in green shadow.
Down the ravine behind the empty house,
The cowbells follow one another
Into the distances of the afternoon.
To my right,
In a field of sunlight between two pines,
The droppings of last year's horses
Blaze up into golden stones.
I lean back, as the evening darkens and comes on.
A chicken hawk floats over, looking for home.
I have wasted my life.

SIR THOMAS WYATT
1503-1542

They flee from me that sometime did me seek

They flee from me that sometime did me seek
  With naked foot stalking in my chamber.
I have seen them gentle, tame and meek
  That now are wild and do not remember
  That sometime they put themselves in danger
To take bread at my hand; and now they range
Busily seeking with a continual change.

Thanked be fortune, it hath been otherwise
  Twenty times better; but once in special,
In thin array after a pleasant guise,
  When her loose gown from her shoulders did fall,
  And she me caught in her arms long and small;
Therewith all sweetly did me kiss,
And softly said, '*Dear heart, how like you this?*'

It was no dream: I lay broad waking.
  But all is turned thorough my gentleness
Into a strange fashion of forsaking,
  And I have leave to go of her goodness,
  And she also to use newfangleness.
But since that I so kindly am served,
I would fain know what she hath deserved.

Full Moon

My bands of silk and miniver
Momently grew heavier;
The black gauze was beggarly thin;
The ermine muffled mouth and chin;
I could not suck the moonlight in.

Harlequin in lozenges
Of love and hate, I walked in these
Striped and ragged rigmaroles;
Along the pavement my footsoles
Trod warily on living coals.

Shouldering the thoughts I loathed,
In their corrupt disguises clothed,
Mortality I could not tear
From my ribs, to leave them bare
Ivory in silver air.

There I walked, and there I raged;
The spiritual savage caged
Within my skeleton, raged afresh
To feel, behind a carnal mesh,
The clean bones crying in the flesh.

W. B. YEATS
1865-1939

Long-Legged Fly

That civilisation may not sink,
Its great battle lost,
Quiet the dog, tether the pony
To a distant post;
Our master Caesar is in the tent
Where the maps are spread,
His eyes fixed upon nothing,
A hand under his head.
Like a long-legged fly upon the stream
His mind moves upon silence.

That the topless towers be burnt
And men recall that face,
Move most gently if move you must
In this lonely place.
She thinks, part woman, three parts a child,
That nobody looks; her feet
Practise a tinker shuffle
Picked up on a street.
Like a long-legged fly upon the stream
Her mind moves upon silence.

That girls at puberty may find
The first Adam in their thought,
Shut the door of the Pope's chapel,
Keep those children out.
There on that scaffolding reclines
Michael Angelo.
With no more sound than the mice make
His hand moves to and fro.
Like a long-legged fly upon the stream
His mind moves upon silence.

Chronological List of Poets

1460-1529	John Skelton
1503-1542	Sir Thomas Wyatt
1539-1577	George Gascoigne
1540-1594	Barnabe Googe
1543-1607	Sir Edward Dyer
1552-1618	Sir Walter Ralegh
1552-1599	Edmund Spenser
1554-1628	Fulke Greville, Lord Brooke
1554-1586	Sir Philip Sidney
1562-1619	Samuel Daniel
1563-1631	Michael Drayton
1564-1616	William Shakespeare
1566-1638	John Hoskins
1567-1620	Thomas Campion
1567-1601	Thomas Nashe
1569-1626	Sir John Davies
1572-1631	John Donne
1572-1637	Ben Jonson
1583-1648	Edward, Lord Herbert of Cherbury
d1586	Chidiock Tichborne
1591-1674	Robert Herrick
1593-1633	George Herbert
1594-1640	Thomas Carew
1606-1687	Edmund Waller
1609-1642	Sir John Suckling

1612-1672 Anne Bradstreet
1618-1667 Abraham Cowley
1618-1657 Richard Lovelace
1621-1678 Andrew Marvell
1627-1656 John Hall
1630-1687 Charles Cotton
1631-1700 John Dryden
1639-1701 Sir Charles Sedley
1640-1689 Aphra Behn
1647-1680 John Wilmot, Earl of Rochester
1667-1745 Jonathan Swift
1688-1744 Alexander Pope
1716-1771 Thomas Gray
1731-1800 William Cowper
1757-1827 William Blake
1759-1796 Robert Burns
1770-1850 William Wordsworth
1772-1834 Samuel Taylor Coleridge
1788-1824 George Gordon, Lord Byron
1792-1822 Percy Bysshe Shelley
1793-1864 John Clare
1795-1821 John Keats
1809-1849 Edgar Allan Poe
1809-1892 Alfred, Lord Tennyson
1812-1889 Robert Browning
1818-1848 Emily Brontë
1819-1861 Arthur Hugh Clough
1819-1892 Walt Whitman
1822-1888 Matthew Arnold
1828-1909 George Meredith
1828-1882 Dante Gabriel Rossetti
1830-1886 Emily Dickinson

1830-1894   Christina Rossetti
1832-1898   Lewis Carroll
1834-1896   William Morris
1837-1909   Algernon Charles Swinburne
1840-1928   Thomas Hardy
1844-1889   Gerard Manley Hopkins
1849-1903   W.E. Henley
1859-1936   A.E. Housman
1865-1936   Rudyard Kipling
1865-1939   W.B. Yeats
1867-1900   Ernest Dowson
1874-1963   Robert Frost
1879-1955   Wallace Stevens
1882-1941   James Joyce
1885-1972   Ezra Pound
1885-1928   Elinor Wylie
1887-1959   Edwin Muir
1887–1964   Edith Sitwell
1888-1965   T.S. Eliot
1888-1974   John Crowe Ransom
1890-1918   Isaac Rosenberg
1892-1950   Edna St. Vincent Millay
1893-1918   Wilfred Owen
1894-1962   e.e. cummings
1895-1986   Robert Graves
1902-1971   Stevie Smith
1906-1984   John Betjeman
1906-1984   William Empson
1907-1973   W.H. Auden
1907-1963   Louis MacNeice
1908-1963   Theodore Roethke
1909-1955   James Agee

1911-1979 Elizabeth Bishop
1913-1966 Delmore Schwartz
1914-1972 John Berryman
1914-1953 Dylan Thomas
1916-1977 Thomas Blackburn
1917-1977 Robert Lowell
1918-1986 W.S. Graham
1922–1986 Philip Larkin
1927-1980 James Wright
1928-1974 Anne Sexton
1932-1963 Sylvia Plath

Index of First Lines

173